INSIDE COMMERCIAL BANKING

INSIDE COMMERCIAL BANKING

ERIC N. COMPTON

Vice President
The Chase Manhattan Bank, N.A.

AMERICAN INSTITUTE OF BANKING

AMERICAN BANKERS ASSOCIATION

1120 Connecticut Avenue, N.W.
Washington, D.C. 20036

A WILEY-INTERSCIENCE PUBLICATION

JOHN WILEY & SONS, New York • Chichester • Brisbane • Toronto

This publication is designed to provide accurate and authoritative information in regard to the subject matter covered. It is sold with the understanding that the publisher is not engaged in rendering legal, accounting, or other professional service. If legal advice or other expert assistance is required, the services of a competent professional person should be sought. *From a Declaration of Principles jointly adopted by a Committee of the American Bar Association and a Committee of Publishers.*

***Library of Congress Cataloging in Publication Data*:**

Compton, Eric N 1925-
Inside commercial banking.

"A Wiley-Interscience publication."
Bibliography: P.
Includes index.
1. Banks and Banking—United States.

2. Banks and banking. 3. Bank management.

I. Title.

HG2491.C644 1980 332.1'2'068 80-13269
ISBN 0-471-07974-X

Printed in the United States of America

10 9 8 7 6 5 4 3 2

To Maire Cathleen, who made it all possible

PREFACE

In Washington a press release announces that in a recent month the federal government initiated almost ten million electronic funds payments to Social Security recipients and armed forces members and that almost two-thirds of these went to commercial bank accounts. In London a senior management task force at one of the largest banks in Great Britain coordinates the details of the takeover of a major New York bank. In Nebraska a husband and wife transfer their savings account from a commercial bank to a savings and loan association that has installed its on-line terminals in a network of local supermarkets; thus they are able to transact their "banking" business directly at the store and may even have the costs of grocery purchases debited to an account at the savings and loan. In Boston a private firm advertises a daily-income money-market fund in which a consumer can buy shares, earn interest on uninvested cash balances left in the fund, and pay bills with check-like instruments drawn against balances and free from per-item service charges. In Chicago one of the nation's largest merchandisers completes plans to offer the public small-denomination savings certificates. In Wilmington a major personal finance company receives approval from the Federal Home Loan Bank Board for its acquisition of a billion-dollar Texas holding company whose principal component is a savings and loan association; the finance company in question already has, as one of its subsidiaries, a Wilmington commercial bank.

All these developments occurred during a single month in 1979. They are cited to illustrate the basic premise that commercial banking in the United States, which has encountered and survived repeated financial crises, is still in a state of constant change in which new forms of competition appear and new challenges are posed to the time-honored, traditional ways of conducting banking business. The student or analyst of our banking system who has become familiar with the chaotic conditions of the Civil War period, the repeated nineteenth-century money crises, the tidal wave of bank failures during the Depression, and the "credit crunches" of both 1974 and 1979 must update his or her knowledge by addressing the topics and issues on the commercial scene. Some of these portend a revolution in the industry that may be at least as dramatic and meaningful as any of the revolutions of the past. The barriers that once separated the various types of financial institutions in America are disappearing. The exclusiveness that commercial banks had long held in many areas no longer exists. Banking is in a state of flux, and to use the term "contemporary" to describe these developments is to run the risk that the next day's news will make the word itself inappropriate.

In 1970, with the full participation and support of New York Chapter of the American Institute of Banking, I prepared a text that provided students of that school with an overview of bank management issues and problems. In 1975 the text was revised to reflect changes that had occurred in the banking system. The state of the art today is such that an entirely new text is called for to create an awareness of the topics that permeate the current banking scene.

Bankers today may be thought of as swimmers in a sea of strong, often divergent currents. Pressures from many directions are exerted on them. Urban activists attack them for not having done enough to solve the problems of the cities. Consumer advocates—perhaps the same people who take advantage of the interest rates offered by banks on purchased money—criticize banks for charging high interest on loans. Human rights advocates demand that banks disassociate themselves completely from countries where civil liberties allegedly have been violated. Law enforcement officers state publicly that banks have been negligent in protecting the assets of customers. Market analysts identify many reasons why commercial bank stocks, as a group, appear unattractive to investors. Competitors continually develop innovative and cost-effective ways of serving a marketplace that was once the banks' tightly held domain. And federal and state governments continually enmesh the banks in an incredible set of restrictive laws and procedures, often creating a situation in which conflicting opinions are rendered by two authorities.

Banking, of course, is by no means alone in complaining about the extent of government regulation today. On the federal level alone, forty-one regulatory agencies employing some 100,000 workers create an annual direct expense of over $5 billion in administrative costs—a figure that does not reflect any of the expenses that private industries must incur in order to meet all the demands of those agencies. In all its aspects, regulation by governments has become an ever-increasing characteristic of American business.[1]

However, although bankers may empathize with their peers in other industries who must comply with so many federal and state regulations, they can justifiably claim that no other business has been subjected to so much control and so many restrictions, many of them overlapping, by such a plethora of authorities and government agencies. The bankers' view has been supported by a former member of the Federal Reserve Board of Governors:

> Banking, with its three federal and fifty state supervisory authorities, and bodies of law to match, is the most overregulated industry in the country.[2]

A commercial bank, in order to open its doors and accept its first deposit, must first undergo a rigorous state or federal chartering process. It cannot merge, open branches, or expand into additional service areas unless government approval is obtained. It is subjected to repeated examinations by federal or state agencies. Its ability to compete with other types of financial institutions is severely limited by various laws. At all times it must tie up funds in segregated reserves, even if such reserves produce no income or direct benefit. In short, nearly every phase of commercial banking is regulated by state and federal laws.

It is for this reason that bankers themselves frequently pose questions that their counterparts in other areas of the economy need not ask. *Why* is it easier for an American commercial bank to open a branch in Singapore than it is for the same bank to open one across the nearest state boundary line? *Why* were foreign banking institutions traditionally given more latitude than domestic banks in their American operations? *Why* have the credit unions and savings and loan associations enjoyed a freedom to function that is often in sharp contrast to the restrictions imposed on commercial banks?

Another recurring problem that bankers must face is that of the *image* of their profession. In an effort to improve that image, they must seek to

[1]Willard C. Butcher, "Onward the Regulation Revolution," (speech at The Commonwealth Club, San Francisco, September 15, 1978).

[2]Henry C. Wallich, "Banks Need More Freedom to Compete," *Fortune*, March 1970, p. 114.

educate the public and to display their concern for customers and communities. Programs are needed to convince government authorities, consumer advocates, minority groups, union leaders, feminists, and environmentalists that the banks are not only acting prudently, but are also actually doing much to meet all the needs of their local communities. Bankers must convey the message that their services are priced properly and that morality and social responsibility are very much a part of their policies and practices.

If there is a single key word in American banking today it is *change.* Technological changes; changes in the manner in which banks fund their growth and price their products; changes in banking legislation; changes in the approach to global banking; and changes in the climate of competition are perhaps the most noticeable. But a corollary of this constant atmosphere of change is the need for a concerted attempt by management to look into the future and develop questions that sum up the major issues and challenges that commercial banks must face. What types of financial institutions will best serve all the needs of each segment of the population? What new technologies and services can be introduced and marketed in a manner palatable to customers? What further changes in federal and state regulations can be anticipated?

In this text, frequent mention is made of the past performance of banks, especially in times of crisis, on the ground that those who ignore history's lessons are condemned to repeat the errors of the past. When mistakes in banking judgment or practice are cited, the intent is not to condemn or to be overly critical of any bank or banker. Today's banks did not become a key element in our trillion-dollar economy by accident or in spite of the caliber of their leaders. Rather their current soundness and profitability flow directly from the diligence and dedication displayed by those previous generations of bankers who identified challenges and problems and developed appropriate responses. Nothing less is called for today. Periods of trial and error may be frustrating and long, but there is reason for hope; banking has coped with many crises in the past, and one must believe it can do so again.

The focus must always be on change. When Stephen Fuller left Harvard's Graduate School of Business Administration to become Vice President in charge of all General Motors personnel, he expressed this thought:

> One of the most significant responsibilities of any management is to make

> sure that the strategies and tactics of the organization are not only perceiving changes, but anticipating them.[3]

His words have at least as much relevance in commercial banking as in the automotive industry. Change *is* intrinsic to the financial picture today. To ignore it is to follow in the footsteps of the dinosaur and the railroads. The traditionalist banker must be aware of the diminished role of his industry in the American marketplace. Commercial banks, which at the close of World War II held more than half of all the assets of the financial services industry , now hold less than 40 percent. [4] Traditional policies may have lost their efficacy with existing and potential customers. Major corporations, which historically depended on commercial banks as a source of credit, bypass them today and use the commercial paper market to the extent of over $100 billion.[5] Sears Roebuck and Company, competing with commercial banks by offering various financial services, generated $420 million in income in 1977 from that source alone—a sum larger than the net income in 1977 of *any* U.S. bank.[6] As of May 1979, 144 foreign banks operated 315 offices in the United States as compared with their 111 offices 6 years earlier, and their assets were 4½ times larger than in 1973; moreover, more than one-half of these banks were operating agencies or branches in more than one state—a privilege denied to American banks.[7]

The commercial banker of bygone days did not have to face these challenges, nor were such terms as point-of-sale terminals, Eurodollar financing, minibranches, OPEC Organization of Petroleum Exporting Countries, and affirmative action in his vocabulary. A "new breed" of commercial banker who, in Dr. Fuller's words, is able to perceive and anticipate change, who is willing to discard the traditional when necessary, and who combines a high sense of awareness of contemporary developments with problem-solving ability, must be developed and motivated.

It is the purpose of this text to identify some of the more important

[3]"GM Zeros in on Employee Discontent," *Business Week*, May 12, 1973.
[4]David Rockefeller, "A Call for Unity," (speech to the American Bankers Association Convention, Honolulu, October 23, 1978).
[5]*Federal Reserve Bulletin*, October 1979, p. A25.
[6]Charles R. Holcomb, "Laissez-Faire Banking,"*Business*, Gannett Newspapers, September 24, 1978.
[7]*Federal Reserve Bulletin*, October 1979, p. 785.

topics and issues that such bankers must be prepared to address today and to discuss the quest for solutions and responses.

John D. MacPhail and John B. Shay, Vice Presidents of The Chase Manhattan Bank, N.A., have been respected associates and have contributed many insights into bank management that are reflected in this text. With deep appreciation, their contributions are acknowledged here.

Francis A. McMullen, Executive Director of the American Institute of Banking's New York Chapter, has supplied unfailing and invaluable support and counsel. His work in reviewing manuscripts and suggesting new approaches to each textbook has been of great assistance, and my sincere thanks go to him.

ERIC N. COMPTON

June 1980
New York, New York

CONTENTS

INSIDE COMMERCIAL BANKING

I

AMERICAN BANKING: A Historical Overview

Because a commercial bank's customers comprise a cross section of individuals, entities of government, businesses, and institutions, the manner in which the bank interfaces with them and provides services to them mirrors the environment. A bank's philosophy, and the extent to which its operations are restricted by laws, can be highly reflective of the outside world. Thus the mood and spirit of the earliest American colonists can be captured and highlighted if one examines the banks they created and the banking system, or lack of one, existing at the time.

When Sir Isaac Newton, in 1687, first promulgated the physical law that for every action there is an equal and opposite reaction, in no way could he have foreseen the applications of that same principle to many areas outside the purview of the sciences. Yet a moment's thought demonstrates that this can be done. An era of strict, prudish morality in society gives way to one of license and vice versa. Fashions go to one extreme, then revert to another. Overly sentimental literary style, romantic literary works, and soft music pass from the scene and are replaced by harsh realism, crude language, and dissonance; the latter, in turn, fade in popularity and a new reaction takes place. So it is with the historical development of the American banking system.

COLONIAL BANKING

The earliest colonists sought independence and personal liberty in all things. Many of them came from countries in which a high degree of government control, affecting many aspects of their daily lives, existed. In those countries, the banking scene was commonly dominated by a strong, central bank and a relative handful of commercial banks. To the colonists this concept was in direct conflict with the broad notion of individual freedom. They reacted by going to the opposite end of the spectrum and applied to banking the same liberties that permitted anyone to follow his or her leanings and open any other type of business.

In direct contrast to the central government banks of England, France, and Sweden, the colonists opted for minimal government supervision. Banks were opened through the granting of a charter by the colony (later, the state or commonwealth), but the requirements for approval of a charter do not appear to have been onerous. Thereafter, examinations of a bank's capital adequacy and prudent operations were infrequent and cursory. The notion of a strong, central unit in the federal government to regulate and examine banks was vigorously opposed, as was any plan for a "national" bank like those in European countries. As geographic areas in the expanding nation opened up for settlement, those individuals who wished to engage in the banking business were almost as free to do so as those who chose other entrepreneurial activities. The same basic concept of freedom that allowed a person to open a tavern, blacksmith's shop, or general store was applied to the formation and operation of a bank.

It required many years for the colonists to accept the fact that the very nature of banking requires a *modus operandi* different from those that prevail in all other industries. Opening and operating a bank cannot be treated on the basis that would be relevant elsewhere. The early settlers do not seem to have recognized the simple truth that a system that allows virtually anyone to open a bank and operate it with little or no regulation and supervision is also a system in which anyone can close a bank. The effect of this insecurity on the overall economy was disastrous. At a time when a sound banking system, in which the public could place its trust, could have contributed greatly to the nation's progress, it was sorely lacking.

The success stories of banks that had their origins in colonial times are few and far between. The original Bank of North America (Philadelphia, 1782) and the Bank of New York and Bank of Massachusetts (both 1784) are notable exceptions in a general history of bank failures and widespread lack of public confidence. Many banks went out of existence because of outright mismanagement, despite what may have been the best of intentions on the part of their organizers; in other cases, the motivation for opening the bank may have lain in the hope of quick profits, followed by hasty departure from the area in order to repeat the process in some new community.

Banks generally hoarded their limited supplies of gold and silver and disbursed loan proceeds by issuing their individual notes to customers. The concept of crediting loan proceeds to a customer's account had not yet taken hold. Each bank's notes presumably were to be used as a medium of exchange, but in actual practice were often rejected by merchants who naturally questioned whether the issuing bank was still in existence. In addition the party to whom these notes were tendered necessarily had to wonder if he would be able to redeem them in hard currency, such as gold or silver, by presenting them to the issuer.

An additional weakness in the colonial banking "system," the ease and prevalence of counterfeiting, created strong feelings of distrust among the merchants to whom bank notes were offered. By the middle of the nineteenth century, over 1500 individual bank note issues were in existence. Printing and circulating bogus notes therefore posed no problem for an enterprising counterfeiter.

For many banks, survival and profitability meant taking all possible measures to discourage or prevent note redemption. A system known as "wildcat banking" evolved in which banks would open note redemption offices at remote locations where only predatory beasts, such as wildcats, supposedly roamed. Noteholders found it difficult, expensive, and time-consuming to travel to such remote sites; thus the banks were able to conserve their precious supplies of gold and silver.

Whenever a colonial bank failed, it left behind a quantity of unredeemable notes in the hands of its customers. Public distrust of the system increased in direct proportion to the number of bank failures and was fueled by the questionable value of any given note. A growing economy and an increasing population clearly exacerbated the need for improvement.

That need was met on two occasions by establishing a new type of financial institution. In both cases a beneficial short-term effect was produced, but the new institutions were legislated out of existence. Both the First and Second Banks of the United States were chartered by Congress in 1791 and 1816, respectively, for 20-year periods. They succeeded in gaining a measure of public confidence because they had the backing of the federal government. However, they also acted as collection agents, accepting from their customers the notes issued by other banks and presenting these for redemption. This "policeman" function was vehemently resented by the other banks and, combined with strong political opposition (including the basic question of the constitutionality of the two banks), provided the rationale in each case for the failure of Congress to renew the charters.

The National Banking Acts

As Secretary of the Treasury under President Abraham Lincoln, Salmon P. Chase was given a mandate to raise the funds necessary for the federal government to continue prosecuting the Civil War and at the same time to devise a solution to the chaotic conditions that existed in the banking system. Two years of conflict between the North and South had created the need for the former; 100 years of virtually unsupervised banking were responsible for the latter. With great ingenuity and diligence, Chase drew up legislation that was passed by Congress in 1863 and amended in 1864. This legislation, which technically consists of both the National Banking and National Currency Acts, is commonly known as the National Bank Act and is a major landmark in American banking history.

The National Bank Act established a new office within the Treasury Department and created the title of Comptroller of the Currency for the individual who was to occupy it. The Comptroller was made responsible for the chartering and supervision of any *national bank*, a new form of financial institution specifically authorized by the Act. To acquire a national bank charter the organizers were required to demonstrate that an adequate supply of initial capital had been raised.

These new banks were empowered to issue a new form of currency, the national bank note. All such notes were uniform in appearance except for the name of the issuer; to insure their acceptance by the public the Act stipulated that a national bank could issue them only if it had purchased an amount of government bonds in proportion to the amount of its capital. If a national bank failed, the Act made each shareholder liable for a sum equal to the value of his holdings in it.

For the first time in American banking history, a system of required reporting and examination came into being. Each national bank was compelled to file with the Comptroller periodic sworn statements of financial condition and was subject to examination by his office at any time. The Act formalized a system of required reserves that were to be maintained for the protection of depositors and indicated the manner in which these could be kept and the geographic locations where reserves were to be domiciled.

In 1865, because existing state-chartered banks displayed little inclination to change their charters and become "national," further legislation was passed, imposing a ten percent federal tax on all issues of state bank notes. This led to a major change in banking practices. To avoid the tax banks began to credit customers' accounts directly with the proceeds of loans.

The Dual Banking System

The National Bank Act was intended to persuade state-chartered banks to convert to national charters. By doing so, they would gain the prestige and public confidence that the latter carried, and since national banks could issue notes only in proportion to their holdings of government bonds, each charter conversion would entail purchases of these obligations and thus contribute to the government's need for funds. In actual practice, however, the state-chartered banks saw little value in joining a system that would require them to maintain higher reserves, restrict their operations, and subject them to periodic audits by the Comptroller of the Currency. For the most part they chose to keep their state charters; hence a *dual* banking system was created that has remained essentially unchanged since 1864. Every commercial bank in the United States must be chartered either by the federal government or the banking department of the state in which it operates. A bank may apply at any time for conversion from one form of charter to the other if it perceives advantages in doing so. Since 1914, although the proportions have varied somewhat from time to time, state-chartered banks have typically accounted for two-thirds of all our commercial banking institutions.[1]

[1] David H. Jones, "The National Banking System: Origins and Objectives," *Banking*, October 1975, p. 146.

A contemporary topic of major concern reflects the increasing frequency of requests by national banks for conversion to state charters. As discussed later, every national bank is required to belong to the Federal Reserve (or "Fed") system and therefore to maintain reserves with it. By converting to a state charter, using correspondent banks to replace the Fed as a source of services, and resigning from the Federal Reserve System, a national bank can avoid tying up those reserves and put the freed-up funds to profitable use.

The Period from 1864 to 1913

The National Bank Act did a great deal to lessen or eliminate the weaknesses that had existed prior to its passage. Its power to charter and examine banks gave the public a new reason for confidence in the soundness of the system. It provided a new, uniform type of currency, the national bank note, known to be backed by government bonds. It gave recognition to the basic principle that banking is, per se, different from other industries and cannot be permitted to function without government supervision and regulation. Indeed, it is difficult or impossible to visualize what might have been the effect on the economy had the abuses and weaknesses of colonial banking been allowed to continue unchecked.

Nevertheless, in retrospect it can be seen that the Act was something far less than a panacea for all the financial ills of an ever-expanding nation. In the years following its passage, significant new weaknesses and problems, either traceable to the Act itself or entirely unforeseen by Salmon Chase and his peers, were identified in the banking system; these attained such proportions that the need for further legislation became apparent.

One such weakness was found in the inflexibility of the nation's money supply. As national banks began to assume an increasingly important role in the economy, their notes became ever more widely accepted as a medium of exchange. To meet the needs of a booming national product and a growing population after the Civil War, an increase in the supply of these notes would have been appropriate and desirable. By law, however, the quantity of national bank notes in circulation was limited to ninety percent of the dollar amount of outstanding government bonds. The supply of notes could not increase unless the government issued additional bonds. A prospering economy naturally made the Treasury more solvent and enabled it to call in for redemption some of the outstanding bond issues, and the quantity of national bank notes necessarily diminished proportionately. This provision of the Act caused the withdrawal from the economy of a nationally accepted form of currency at the very time when it was most needed.

A second weakness resulted from the provision of the Act that called for national banks to maintain a specified base of reserves in money center cities, the largest of which was New York. No provision was made in the Act for seasonal fluctuations in reserves; the same requirements applied at all times. In a pyramid effect, reserves from banks throughout the system concentrated in New York. Banks in that city naturally put the funds to work in the form of loans and investments. When they were called upon to release any of the reserves to the banks that occupied lower positions in the pyramid, they were forced to meet their obligation by selling some of their investments or calling in loans. Either action was highly undesirable from the standpoint of goodwill with customers and detrimental from the standpoint of profits; forced sales of securities often produced less than the desired return, and forced liquidation of loans often resulted in direct losses.

The third defect in the National Bank Act, as subsequently perceived, lay in its failure to make any provision for the speedy presentation and collection of checks throughout the country. As the population grew and commerce increased, the check became more widely used as a payment medium; however, no thought was given to ways in which the process of delivering checks to their drawee banks and obtaining settlement for them could be expedited. Checks drawn on out-of-town banks were typically collected through a correspondent, but the process, whether by design or through its inherent weakness, was slow and cumbersome. It was not uncommon for weeks to elapse before a deposited check was finally converted into usable, collected funds.

Recognition of the need for further reform in the banking system and for corrective legislation to address these three fundamental weaknesses was triggered by the depression of 1893 and the financial panic in 1907 in which several banks were forced to close their doors. A National Monetary Commission was named to submit ideas for financial reform to Congress, and a series of hearings held by the House Banking and Currency Committee examined the state of the nation's financial resources. An American Bankers Association committee, agrarian leaders, the presidents of forty-seven state banking associations, spokesmen for both progressive and conservative factions, and President Woodrow Wilson himself all contributed ideas and exerted influence. After extensive compromise sessions between the Senate and House, the Federal Reserve Act, which reflected the input of many of the abovementioned groups, was signed into law by Wilson in December 1913[2]

THE FEDERAL RESERVE ACT

Like the legislation of 1863, which had stemmed directly from the crises and weaknesses of colonial and nineteenth-century banking, the Federal Reserve Act resulted from the government's recognition of the need for reforming and strengthening the system. It has been characterized as the greatest single piece of legislation, aside from wartime measures, of the Wilson years.[3] The Act represents a blend of elements that were incorporated into it as a means of satisfying the demands of many diverse groups. To those who opposed a strong central bank and resented any form of increased government control, it offered the proviso that the Federal Reserve would be privately owned. To those who feared an expansion of power, in that either the President or the Congress or both might be in a position to dictate to the banks, it made the Federal Reserve independent of both and thus conferred on it an autonomy that still exists. To all the bankers who had expressed fears about the degree of control that the Fed might be able to exercise over their banking operations, the Act offered a compromise: all national banks would be required to join, whereas membership would be optional for state-chartered banks. To those who had pointed out the weaknesses in the banking system that had developed since 1864, it specifically offered viable solutions.

The Federal Reserve Act stipulated that members in the new system would be required to buy stock in it in an amount equal to 6 percent of their capital and surplus. It divided the nation into twelve geographic districts and established a Federal Reserve Bank in each; these twelve district banks would serve as the repositories for the reserves that member banks had to maintain and would also provide facilities for the rapid

[2]The step-by-step progress of the Act is detailed by Roger T. Johnson in *Historical Beginnings: The Federal Reserve*, Boston, Federal Reserve Bank of Boston, 1977.
[3]"The Coming of the Fed," *Banking*, October 1975, p. 148.

and efficient collection of checks—thus solving two of the fundamental weaknesses of the post-1864 era. The issuance of Federal Reserve notes as a form of legal tender was authorized, and the Fed in each district was also empowered to act as the distributor of currency and coin to be supplied to member banks.

Federal Reserve Banks were given responsibility for the safekeeping, issuance, and redemption of all U.S. government obligations. The Fed was authorized to conduct examinations of all its member banks, to issue regulations governing their operations, to operate the federal government's checking accounts, and to control the national flow of money and credit through a variety of techniques. These techniques form the foundation for much of today's monetary policy in the United States.

When the Federal Reserve's Board of Governors wishes to make bank credit more difficult to obtain, it can increase the reserve requirements for member banks. By compelling them to maintain larger reserves with it, the Fed decreases their loanable funds. If the Fed raises the *discount rate*—the interest paid by member banks when they borrow from it—it can make borrowing less attractive to them and ultimately cause them to raise their own interest rates within statutory limits. Finally, through its Open Market Operations it can sell additional government obligations, thus taking money out of circulation. If the Board of Governors wishes to make bank credit easier to obtain and to increase the nation's money supply, it can implement changes in the opposite direction in any or all of these three areas.

During 1977 and 1978 the number of commercial banks in the United States fluctuated from a low of 14,689 to a high of 14,721. Throughout that period the number of Fed member banks never exceeded 5669, and the System showed a net *loss* in membership of sixty-eight banks in 1978.[4] Although membership in the Federal Reserve is held by less than half of all commercial banks, those institutions that are members control total demand and time deposits of over $716 billion, or approximately 72 percent of the total deposits in the system.[5]

As mentioned earlier, the desirability of Fed membership has become a contemporary topic of increased importance. Granted that the Fed performs many useful services for its members, such as collecting checks for them, supplying them with coin and currency, making its credit

[4] *Federal Reserve Bulletin*, January 1979, p. A17.
[5] *Ibid.*, p. A17.

facilities available to them, and providing a nationwide wire transfer system to which they have access; and granted that it has always offered these on a free basis (except for interest charged on loans), many national banks nevertheless withdrew from the Fed in 1977 and 1978 by applying for state charters. Their motivation for this action rests chiefly on the provision of the Federal Reserve Act pertaining to reserve requirements. Since December 1976, all member banks with demand deposits in excess of $400 million have been required to maintain reserves of 16¼ percent at their district Federal Reserve Bank.[6] If these funds were not tied up in reserves at the Fed, earning no interest, they could obviously be put to immediate use by the banks in their continuing effort to meet customers' demands for credit. Each escalation in interest rates exacerbates this problem. In 1978 Walter Wriston, Chairman of Citibank, N.A., estimated that his bank could generate annual pretax earnings of $80 to $90 million if its reserves at the Fed were freed up and loaned out[7]; the very significant increases in money market rates that have occurred since 1975 would indicate that today's estimate would be considerably higher.

Every withdrawal of a bank from the Fed system is viewed as causing a weakening of the Federal Reserve's capability to control the flow of money and credit. The smaller the number of commercial banks that fall under its jurisdiction, the less influential the Federal Reserve can be in exercising its powers and its perceived responsibilities. One possible compromise has been suggested.

Legislation was proposed in 1979 to have member banks pay direct fees to the Fed for all the services they obtain; in exchange, the Fed would pay them interest on their reserve account balances above a specified dollar amount. At this writing, the net effect on Federal Reserve earnings (which amounted to $10.3 billion in 1979, a 22 percent increase over those of the previous year[8]) has not been calculated.

The range of Federal Reserve actions as they affect member banks and the nation's economy is enormous. A random sampling from Fed publications provides some indication of the importance of the steps taken in 1978 by the Board of Governors. In addition to the weekly decisions that had to be made regarding purchases or sales of govern-

[6] *Ibid.*, p. A9.

[7] In "Banking in Transition," *The Bankers Magazine*, September-October 1978, p. 35.

[8] *Federal Reserve Bulletin*, January 1980, p. 32.

ment obligations, the Fed issued new regulations pertaining to payment of interest on time and savings deposits, authorized the issuance of a new form of money market certificate, acted to strengthen the dollar in foreign exchange markets, handed down decisions in seven cases involving applications for the formation of new bank holding companies or for the offering of new services by existing holding companies, and adopted guidelines for the implementation of Truth in Lending regulations. During 1979 the Fed calendar was even more crowded, and its decisions even more momentous, as a result of the year's events: conditions in the money market, efforts to curb inflation, OPEC actions, and the increased activities of foreign banks on the domestic scene.

What has the Fed done for the commercial banking system? It has resolved the problems of "pyramid" reserves, check collection, and money supply. It has brought much-needed strength to the bank examination process. Recently, it has served its members as a lender of last resort—the source of credit that can be used when the capacities of all others have been exhausted. A noteworthy example of this occurred when Penn Central's bankruptcy (1960) led to a potential collapse in the nationwide commercial paper market. By providing unqualified assurance to its members that it would supply funds, the Federal Reserve averted a fiscal crisis of major proportions.

The independence of the Fed from Congress and the White House and the lack of agreement among many authorities as to the wisdom of its monetary policy actions are among the factors that continue to make it a controversial, as well as highly visible, agency. As with the National Bank Act, however, the Federal Reserve Act was so necessary that one cannot visualize a banking system and an economy that could have grown and profited without it.

Federal Deposit Insurance Corporation

With the Federal Reserve System in place and the economy on a peacetime basis after World War I, America embarked on an era of unrestrained optimism and rapid economic growth. Commercial banks both reflected and participated in the vitality of the Roaring Twenties. Stock market averages soared, businesses of every type reported record profits, and individuals became more affluent, at least in terms of paper values. Federal and state authorities liberalized their criteria for chartering and permitted many new banks to open, perhaps assuming that these could not fail to benefit from the nation's economic boom. The banks, in turn, capitalized on existing laws and became active underwriters of new securities issues while building up their portfolios through heavy investments in common stocks. Interbank competition for new sources of funds intensified, and banks vied with one another in offering interest on demand deposits as a means of attracting new customers.

Just as the authors of the 1863 Act could not have foreseen the problems that made its subsequent reform necessary, Wilson and his colleagues could not have predicted the tragic events of the Depression era. The interrelationship between banks and their economic environment is nowhere more apparent than during this period. The collapse of the stock market in October 1929 marked the end of the boom period, and those banks that had been quick to take advantage of the climate of unbridled optimism, and in many cases had contributed to it, began to suffer dreadful reverses.

Bank failures during the years from 1920 to 1929 had averaged about 550 per year; in 1930, following the stock market crash, over 1300 banks were forced to cease operating as their loan and investment losses mounted.[9] The "domino effect" of a single bank failure has often been noted; when over 1000 banks fail in one year, a crisis is inevitable as fear sweeps through the population and widespread attempts by depositors to convert deposits into currency take place.

Public confidence, already low, suffered further when the Bank of the United States, with over $200 million in deposits, was forced to close at the end of 1930. This was the largest bank failure in history and intensified the fiscal crisis because the bank name led many individuals to believe that it was the official bank for the government. The Fed found its prestige damaged by its inability to keep the bank from failing. America's financial panic soon spread abroad as Great Britain and twenty-five other countries abandoned the gold standard. During 1932 an additional 2000 commercial banks, with over $1.7 billion in deposits, failed,[10] and the surviving banks drastically curtailed their credit facilities. As businesses found themselves unable to borrow, they were forced to close, and unemployment reached the incredible level of 25 percent. Bank loans, which had totalled $36 billion in 1929, shrank to $11 billion by 1933, and when supplies of money and credit were most sorely

[9]Frances E. Wrocklage, "Banking in the Depression," *Banking*, October 1975, p. 40.
[10]*Ibid.*, pp. 41-42.

needed, they simply were not available. Because Fed membership was mandatory only for national banks, that agency was powerless in the majority of cases; in 1930 there were 17,026 state banks not supervised by any federal agency, and many of these were among the failures.[11] At the end of a 5-year period (1929 through 1933), the record showed that over $7 billion in deposits had been lost through over 9000 bank failures.[12]

President Franklin D. Roosevelt, in one of his first official acts following his inauguration in March 1933, shut down the entire banking system for several days. This was intended to provide a cooling-off period during which the banks could reorganize and the panic could subside. Congress immediately began a series of hearings, which culminated in the 1933 statutes that reformed the system.

Under the Glass-Steagall Act banks were no longer allowed to underwrite municipal revenue bonds. Additional legislation prohibited banks from investing in any common stocks for their own portfolios.

The 1933 Banking Act created the Federal Deposit Insurance Corporation (FDIC) as an official agency of the federal government, organized with the objectives of protecting depositors at banks and promoting safe and sound banking practices. All Fed member banks were required to join the FDIC; state-chartered nonmembers and mutual savings banks were invited to do so. The orginal insurance limit of $2500 per depositor has repeatedly been increased and is now $100,000.

FDIC operations are supervised by a three-person Board of Governors, two of whom are appointed by the President. The Comptroller of the Currency is the third member, *ex officio*. The Corporation's rights and powers include:

1. Setting standards for its member banks.
2. Examining them.
3. Setting maximum interest rates for any FDIC members not otherwise regulated.
4. Ruling on merger or branching requests from member banks.
5. Causing the removal of any director, officer, or management member who is deemed to have violated regulations or statutes or to have engaged in unsound banking practices.

[11] Herbert V. Prochnow and Herbert V. Prochnow, Jr. (Eds), *The Changing World of Banking*, New York, Harper & Row, 1974, p. 74.
[12] Wrocklage, *op. cit.*, p. 150.

6. Issuing cease-and-desist orders as a means of correcting identified weaknesses in member banks.
7. Taking remedial action to assist a member bank that is in difficulty.
8. Providing insurance coverage, within specified limits, for depositors at member institutions.

The remedial actions that the FDIC may take include directly loaning to a bank, purchasing assets from it, depositing funds with it, and effecting its merger with a stronger institution. The FDIC maintains and continually updates a "problem list," which included 342 banks at year-end 1978.[13] At that time, 97 percent of all commercial and mutual savings banks were members, and a deposit insurance fund of $8.8 billion existed for the protection of depositors.[14]

The FDIC is authorized to borrow up to $3 billion at any time from the U.S. Treasury, but even when the two largest bank failures in American history occurred[15] this borrowing privilege was never exercised. All FDIC members must pay annual assessments of 1⁄12 of 1 percent on deposits as a form of insurance premium. When the operating results warrant it, as has been true in every year since 1950, the FDIC refunds a portion of this annual assessment to the banks.

THE BANKING STRUCTURE TODAY

Perhaps the most striking single characteristic of the American banking system today is diversification. In other nations four or five major commercial banks dominate the scene; here, over 14,000 function. This diversification reflects the views of the colonists, who espoused unlimited competition under the system of free enterprise. Their ideals formed the basis for the "free banking" laws that were passed in many states in the nineteenth century. These laws reflected a deep, widely held concern over the possible concentration of economic power in a small number of banks and the ill effects of centralization of authority in a federal agency. Thomas Jefferson considered any form of a central or national bank an invasion of states' rights and a violation of the spirit and letter

[13]Federal Deposit Insurance Corporation, *Annual Report of Operations*, Washington, DC, 1978, p. 3.

[14]*Ibid.*

[15]Franklin National Bank (New York) and United States National Bank (San Diego), both in 1974.

of the Constitution; Alexander Hamilton, on the other hand, believed that it was the federal government's duty to intervene whenever necessary for the protection of a public that would not always act according to reason and justice.[16] The chaotic conditions that "free banking" helped to create provided the justification for the National Bank Act.

Similarly, it was only as a result of the problems and weaknesses in the banking system—the pyramiding of reserves, the lack of a flexible money supply, and the absence of a nationwide program for efficient and quick collection of checks—that the Federal Reserve was created. Wilson himself recognized this and made the subject of banking and currency reform part of his 1912 presidential campaign.

Again, it was only as a result of the crisis of the Depression years that the FDIC came into being. The widespread lack of public confidence caused by several thousand bank failures, with the consequent loss of billions of dollars to depositors, triggered the 1933 Banking Act.

This brief overview of the historical evolution of our present banking system, then, admittedly pays more attention to the problems and failures than to the successes. It stresses the crises, panics, weaknesses, and unstable financial conditions as the causative factors.

The rational for this emphasis on the negative aspects of our banking history lies in the learning process that looks back on the past and attempts to apply its lessons to the present. Our current system of chartering, supervising, and examining commercial banks has been strongly criticized in recent years as duplicative, overly restrictive, and lacking in ability to respond to thc changing needs of banks in a highly competitive environment. At the same time it has been justified on the grounds that it is intended to prevent banks from making the mistakes that led to failures in the past; and if, in fact, overregulation exists, the banker's resentment of it must be tempered by the realization that the degree of public trust that banks seek to enjoy, and the impact of their operations on the nation's economy, are such that they cannot be given the same latitude extended to other businesses.[17]

At the same time, banks have this in common with other industries: their effectiveness can be judged by their ability to recognize weaknesses

[16]Diane G. McConnell, "Central Banking in the New Nation," *Banking*, October 1975, pp. 34-35.

[17]Howard D. Crosse and George H. Hempel, *Management Policies for Commercial Banks*, 2nd ed., Englewood Cliffs, NJ, Prentice-Hall, 1973, p. 18.

and problems and to respond to these promptly and effectively. Much of the legislation affecting banking in the past resulted from the banks' failure to initiate corrective action. It is hoped that today's bankers are being trained, developed, and motivated to follow a different course and thus to serve banking in a more professional manner. They may never enjoy the degree of freedom that their predecessors had, but bemoaning that fact is fruitless. Rather, they must be problem-oriented and prepared to contribute to the nation's well-being, even within a framework of externally imposed constraints. A synergy of all the factors constituting effective management is necessary if that contribution is to be made.

One quality that will make the banker more effective is an ability on his or her part to consider banking in terms of its need to meet a set of obligations to various constituencies. For some of these obligations, no precedent can be found because they did not exist in the past. In other cases, the obligation may have theoretically existed but went unrecognized and therefore unsatisfied. In today's banking this concept of a set of obligations that directly affect the bank's management approach, its range of services, and its daily operations may be considered essential to the growth and profitability of the industry and its components—the banks themselves.

II

THE CONSTITUENCIES OF COMMERCIAL BANKS

The individuals who supply the capital needed to form a new company, produce a Broadway play, or fund a research project find that the process is relatively simple. By executing the appropriate legal documents and issuing checks as their contributions to the new project, they meet the basic requirements and need do little more. When a group applies for a charter for a new bank, however, additional and very different procedures are required. The organizers of a new bank must be prepared to prove to federal and/or state authorities that there is a need for it in its area, that they have adequate capital, and that they are of unimpeachable character and have a record of expertise and success in their own careers. They are also expected to demonstrate the likelihood of growth and profitability for the new institution.

In short, the previously expressed theme repeats itself: banking *is* different from all other industries, and its inherent obligations to various groups can be identified from the outset.

Martin Mayer[1] has noted that the free enterprise system gives any individual the unquestioned right to open the business of his or her choice except when the formation of a bank is at issue. It is the very topic of obligations that makes this observation valid. Our commercial

[1] *The Bankers*, New York, David McKay Co., 1974, p. 67.

banks are part of the private sector, owned by many investors. The bank owes its origin to its *stockholders*, and these constitute the first group to which certain definite obligations exist.

Because commercial banks have the unique ability to "create" money by approving loans and crediting the proceeds to accounts, thus increasing the money supply; because banking as an industry is so important to the national economy; and because commercial banks hold some three-quarters of the money supply (M_1) in the form of demand deposits, federal and state *governments* have a deep concern for the soundness of the system and the policies and practices of banks in general. These agencies of government impose obligations on each bank.

Depositors, and the *public* in general, form a third constituency for commercial banks. They expect certain levels of performance and certain services which must be provided on an efficient, prompt, and cost-effective basis. The bank must project an image of solidity and safety at all times.

Most banks today have embarked on entirely new approaches to the question of personnel management. This reflects recognition of their obligations to the *staff*, both official and clerical.

Finally, banks, like most corporations, now find themselves ever more deeply involved in questions of social responsibility. These were never previously considered subjects for concern. Banks today are in the spotlight in terms of meeting their obligations to the *community*.

The effective bank is the one that recognizes these obligations and fulfills them; the bank that pays no attention to any of them is destined for a short and unprofitable existence.

STOCKHOLDERS

Individuals who buy bank stocks generally accept the essential conservatism of the industry and do not expect their holdings to match the growth record in the marketplace of the more glamorous and exotic stocks. This generalization traditionally has been offset by another, which holds that bank stocks are not subject to the same wide fluctuations as those seen in other industries.

A third generalization may be made, supported by stock market analyses. There appears to be a lack of confidence among investors regarding the banks' ability to meet contemporary challenges and generate adequate profits. Hence although a price/earnings ratio of 10 is considered a norm in the marketplace, it does not apply to bank stocks. Shares in the major bank holding companies can generally be purchased today at prices five or six times annual earnings. Significant swings in per-share prices are rare, even when banks report major improvements in quarterly earnings.

In an age of consumerism, "sunshine laws," and full disclosure, bank stockholders display a far greater tendency than before to be inquisitive and vocal regarding all phases of the institution's performance and activities. The bank can no longer satisfy its obligation to them by simply reporting increased profits. Today it must be prepared to answer their questions regarding lending policies in nations accused of civil rights violations, incentive plans and expense accounts for senior officers, political contributions, and new security measures that may have been taken in reaction to the publicized problems of other banks. Like the annual stockholders' meetings, the published annual reports of banks have become far lengthier as more charts and graphics, 5- and 10-year comparative summaries, detailed statements of policy and practices, and biographies of officers appear.

GOVERNMENTS

A bank's obligations to federal and state agencies can be summarized far more succinctly. These agencies will take all possible steps to assure that every bank is operating prudently and in conformity with all appropriate laws and regulations. Whenever a bank is examined by a government agency, a full report of the examiners' findings is sent to the directors with suggestions for any remedial action that may be necessary. The Comptroller of the Currency, Federal Reserve, FDIC, and state banking departments may issue cease-and-desist orders whenever they find a bank engaging in unsound practices, and they can cause the removal from office of an officer or director who has been deemed guilty of contributing to these. Repeated violations or management shortcomings result in the closing of the bank by government fiat and the assumption of its assets and liabilities by another bank or by an entity of government itself (e.g., the FDIC). In the abstract a bank is obligated to know, understand, and implement all the statutes affecting it because only in this way can the interests of all parties be served. In concrete terms a bank is obligated to do so because it will not be allowed to continue operating if it does not.

DEPOSITORS

Depositors expect transactions to be handled promptly, courteously, and accurately, and must be made to feel that their funds are protected with the utmost care. They look to their banks as a prime source of credit and consider that their relationship gives them the right to call on the bank in time of need. They expect the bank to make it convenient and easy for them to conduct their financial transactions and recognize that they have more freedom of choice in this respect than ever before. A bank that offers a limited range of services, and does not price them competitively, is doomed to lose customers to other financial institutions that are steadily assuming a larger share of the total marketplace.

Beyond these basics the public often expects a banker to serve as a consultant on financial matters of all types. Legal opinions, predictions of economic trends, aid in drawing up wills, and investment advice are often sought, and it may be difficult for the banker to explain why these requests cannot be met.

STAFF

The attitude of stockholders, the requirements of governments, and the expectations of depositors have all undergone changes in recent years, but the dynamics of change are nowhere more apparent than in the area of human resources management. The very term "human resources" is indicative of this change; it is now used instead of "personnel" to reflect the bank's awareness that the staff is a resource of the organization just as its deposits, technology, and assets are. Banks today accept an entirely new set of obligations to their staff members. Their programs of recruiting and training, salary and fringe benefit administration, job enrichment, performance reviews, and supervisory and sensitivity training exemplify this.

The board of directors, in any bank or corporate structure, is the active, governing body at the apex of the organization. It is logical to expect, therefore, that the best method of identifying a bank's obligations to all its constituencies is by giving them some voice on the board. This is exactly what has happened during the 1970s. Board membership at major banks is now held by, among others, female attorneys, clergymen, and members of minority groups who in previous years would never have been candidates for such roles. The goal is to have these individuals bring new insights to board discussions—insights that might never have been contributed by the select hierarchy from which bank directors were traditionally drawn.

Another aspect of change in the staffing picture has resulted from discarding the provincialism and parochialism displayed by bankers in the past. Those attitudes led them to believe that they alone could solve the problems of banks. Today it is commonplace for management to recruit actively from other disciplines and industries. Specialists in such fields as systems analysis, cost accounting, data processing, financial controls and training have been added to the staffs of major banks to bring with them an expertise that the institutions themselves could not provide.

Bankers have also displayed a drastic change in their thinking vis-à-vis the entry-level skills, life-styles, and attitudes of staff members. New questions are being posed as to the validity of past requirements and management techniques. Must each new employee display the level of educational attainment that banks formerly demanded? Is a criminal record an absolute barrier to any type of employment in a bank, as it once was?[2] Can officers, managers, and supervisors interact with subordinates on a purely authoritarian basis, as they traditionally have? Candidates for bank employment today place far less emphasis on the security and prestige of the job and are well aware of other opportunities. They look for immediate benefits rather than the long-range attractiveness of pension and deferred compensation plans.

Similar attitudinal changes prevail among those who seek management positions. They look for jobs that will offer them decision-making opportunities as quickly as possible and display a far greater degree of mobility than their predecessors; if the organization fails to meet their expectations they have no hesitation in leaving it.[3]

Banks necessarily devote a great deal of money and time to the main-

[2]Chemical New York Corporation (*Annual Report*, 1973) reported on a special program for hiring ex-convicts.

[3]Interviews with John Haynes and Nathan Glassman, National Committee on Employment of Youth, in *New Generation*, 52(4), New York, 1970.

enance of computers and other inanimate resources. Certainly no less expense and effort should be dedicated to the "maintenance" of the organization's most important component, its workers. The emphasis on production efficiency always exists, but what has now been added to it is a realization that no degree of mechanization or automation will ever eliminate the human element that makes efficiency possible.[4] The work of Abraham Maslow, Frederick Herzberg, and Douglas McGregor reflects this thinking,[5] and in analyzing the nature and attitudes of employees they suggest management approaches that can create better relationships, resulting in better achievement of goals. The theories of these three individuals have now been incorporated into the human resources management programs at many banks.

Terms such as "motivation," "job enrichment," "career pathing," and "participatory management" have now become part of the banker's vocabulary as new and different obligations to the staff are identified. Programs that combine job functions, allow employees freedom to innovate, and permit decision making at lower levels have been successfully implemented in banking,[6] and other programs have been introduced for the benefit of minority group members to address their value systems, culture, and aspirations.[7]

Affirmative Action

High on the list of contemporary topics in the area of human resources management is the need for specific action to eliminte all forms of discrimination. Historically the American banking industry has been dominated by white, native-born, Protestant males,[8] but the traditional barriers began to crumble during World War II as women began to assume many tasks that had previously been consigned only to men. Later, the Civil Rights Act of 1964, supplemented by legislation in 1967 prohibiting discrimination based on age and by subsequent Presidential

[4]William M. Berliner, *Managerial and Supervisory Practice: Cases and Principles*, 7th ed., Homewood, IL, Richard D. Irwin, 1979, p. 488.

[5]See the bibliography for specific works by Maslow, Herzberg, and McGregor.

[6]"Bankers Trust Broadens Jobs to Improve Efficiency and Morale," *American Banker*, March 19, 1973. Other, unpublished interviews support this.

[7]Berliner, *op. cit.*, p. 368.

[8]Robert M. Fulmer, *Practical Human Relations*, Homewood, IL, Richard D. Irwin, 1977, p. 365.

Executive Orders 11141 and 11246, provided the impetus. As is evidenced by the most recent Conference Board report, banks have now assumed a leading position among all industries in complying with Equal Employment Opportunity goals.[9] Federal government statistics disclose that women and minorities have at least doubled their representation among bank managers and officers since 1970.[10] Major banks today have prepared and implemented detailed affirmative action plans, subject to regular audit by various levels of government, that spell out their antidiscrimination practices; in accordance with the regulations of the Office of Federal Contract Compliance (OFCC), these plans include information on the steps taken by the bank to attain the goal of full equality in all respects for all employees.[11]

COMMUNITIES

American business history is replete with tales of companies that routinely polluted the environment, acted unethically in forcing competitors out of the way, and ignored health and safety standards for their staff members. The job of management consisted exclusively of achieving profits,[12] and the tycoon who said, "The public be damned!" had many counterparts to whom the concept of social and civic responsibility meant little or nothing.

The twentieth century, conversely, especially in the 1970s, has become known as the age of consumerism and protest and as the period during which pressure for socially responsible actions has steadily increased. Corporate policies and procedures today are subject to critical analysis by stockholders (who are far more vocal and numerous than before), consumer advocates (who have become far more visible in society), entities of government (who profess to act in the public interest), the media, and a host of activist groups. It no longer suffices for any bank or business simply to point to its bottom-line successes. Corpora-

[9] Daniel Cowles, "Banks Top Industry in EEOC Compliance," *American Banker*, May 4, 1979, p. 2.

[10] J. Veronica Biggins, "Banks Show Significant Progress for Women and Minorities," *ABA Banking Journal*, September 1979, p. 22.

[11] The OFCC oversees the employment practices of nonconstruction companies with fifty or more employees and with federal contracts for $50,000 or more.

[12] Robert M. Fulmer, *The New Management*, 2nd ed., New York, Macmillan, 1978, p. 259.

tions are expected to employ their skills to improve the quality of life for all citizens,[13] and there is widespread demand for businesspersons to make social concerns a matter of paramount importance.[14]

Commercial banks are subject to at least the same pressures as other businesses in this regard; and in many cases they find themselves called on to display even more social responsibility than their corporate peer group. This pressure is usually based on the premise that banks operate with money taken from the community; hence they should be expected to invest in the community in a variety of tangible forms. Supporting the local Little League or Chamber of Commerce, or having officers serve on hospital or school boards, is no longer sufficient. The former Chairman of Bank of America has pointed out that banks and businesses no longer enjoy their former privilege of merely providing those programs that are implemented

> with one eye on . . . self-interest. Those in corporate life are going to be expected to do things for the good of society just to earn their franchise, their corporate right to exist.[15]

Yet there is an element of self-interest in each program of social responsibility that a bank introduces, simply because the growth and profitability of the institution are closely tied to those of the community in which it operates. If a town or city displays symptoms of urban decay and blight, other businesses may move away; banks lack this option and rise or fall as their communities do. One of the nation's largest banks has stated this as a matter of corporate policy:

> The well-being of the environment in which a bank functions economically and socially is critical to its profitability, and therefore to the discharge of stockholder responsibility. Both are very dependent on each other.[16]

Social responsibility, therefore, has become a recognized obligation of the banks; yet it cannot be viewed in isolation and without regard to the

[13] *Ibid.* p. 441.

[14] Peter F. Drucker (Ed.), *Preparing Tomorrow's Business Leaders Today*, Englewood Cliffs, NJ, Prentice-Hall, 1969, p. 77.

[15] In *Future Without Shock* by Louis B. Lundborg, Copyright © 1974 by W. W. Norton & Company, Inc., New York, NY, p. 84. Reprinted by permission.

[16] Chemical New York Corporation, *Annual Report*, 1977.

other obligations inherent in the business. Their actions may not be immediately compatible with profit objectives. David Rockefeller, in addressing this question, has pointed out that living up to its social responsibilities may be even more significant for a bank than maximizing profits.[17] Indeed, fears have been expressed in some quarters that the latter goal may be neglected if banks and businesses overreact to social and community pressures. Milton Friedman, for example, has been quoted as saying that the "social responsibility of business *is* to increase profits,"[18] and he foresees dire consequences for the economy of a free society if the profit motive becomes secondary to the notion of social responsibility.[19] Programs that banks undertake for the benefit of the community may entail significant expenditures. One major commercial bank published a list of over 200 contributions it had made in a single year to environmental protection groups, educational institutions, neighborhood projects, cultural organizations, and housing and redevelopment associations; it announced that 2 percent of its aftertax earnings would be allocated to this ongoing program of social responsibility.[20] This information was disseminated to all stockholders.

Thus although social consciousness may be viewed as an absolute necessity and a direct obligation for banks, it requires a delicate balance to keep it within the context of overall profitability. An outstanding record as a corporate citizen will not necessarily guarantee liquidity and profits, but conversely a bank that is unwilling to take socially responsible actions because of their effect on profits can be the target not only for public criticism, but also for some form of reprisals.

Motivation

Whenever a highly visible business adopts a plan of social action, questions may be raised about its reasons for doing so. Does a bank act in a socially responsible way because this is the correct course to follow, because it realizes its options are limited, or because one of its branches has been burned by militants who oppose its bigness and view it as a hostile element of the establishment?[21] Does a major corporation discontinue

[17] *Creative Management in Banking*, New York, McGraw-Hill, 1964, p. 83.
[18] In Lundborg, *op. cit.*, p. 81 (emphasis added).
[19] In Fulmer, *The New Management*, p. 444.
[20] The Chase Manhattan Corporation, *Philanthropic Activities: 1978*, New York, 1979.
[21] Lundborg, *op. cit.*, pp. 20–21.

polluting because it is a good citizen, because it gains tax benefits by installing new equipment, or because it fears its sales will drop through adverse publicity? Expediency and altruism often go hand in hand; cynical questions may be posed, and motives are not always readily discernible.[22]

For many banks, the answers will frequently be found in a combination of factors, including the following:

1. Government regulations.
2. Direct pressure from various groups.
3. Voluntary commitments.

Government Regulations. Federal, state, and local laws require equality of opportunity in all phases of a bank's personnel practices. Evidence of discrimination in hiring or promoting may lead to penalties of substantial fines or exclusion from all account relationships and other dealings with government entities. Similar antidiscriminatory laws apply to lending. The forms used in the loan process, and the techniques used in collecting loans, must conform to government regulations so that the rights of minorities are protected.

More recently, the Community Reinvestment Act, passed by Congress in November 1978, has created a direct obligation for all financial institutions to meet the credit needs of their neighborhoods. Whenever the Comptroller of the Currency, Federal Reserve Board, or FDIC is considering a request from a commercial bank or insured savings bank for a charter, merger, new branch, acquisition, or holding company activity, the decision made by that agency must give effect to all that the bank has done or failed to do in meeting community needs. The Federal Home Loan Bank Board must be guided by the same legislation in dealing with savings and loan associations. The basic premise of the Act is that institutions that have not done enough for their communities should be enjoined from further growth. Comments pro or con a bank's lending policies and practices are invited from the public, and all such comments become part of the institution's dossier, on file with each regulatory agency.

The Act was a response by Congress to the many charges of "redlin-

[22] Richard J. C. Roeber, *The Organization in a Changing Environment*, Reading, MA, Addison-Wesley, 1973, p. 115.

ing" that have been brought against financial institutions. This pejorative term describes the policy allegedly followed in drawing boundaries in red ink on a map, delineating areas in which mortgage loans are not to be considered.[23] Prior to passage of the Act fifteen lawsuits had been brought by civic groups against federal regulatory bodies, charging them with failure to comply with the 1964 Civil Rights Act. By compelling those agencies to consider any charges of redlining in their decision-making process, the Community Reinvestment Act may prevent litigation of this type.[24]

Irate civic groups in an area of New York City led a movement that resulted in the withdrawal of over $600,000 in deposits from a bank that had been charged with systematic redlining. They contended that the bank, having received deposits from the community, should reinvest those funds in it. Subsequently the same bank found its application for an additional branch site rejected by the FDIC Board of Governors on the ground of redlining.[25]

Many questions have been raised regarding the provisions of the Community Reinvestment Act. Two sets of supplementary information have already been drawn up and published[26]; it appears, however, that even more clarification is needed to define "credit needs" in a more exact manner and to spell out the extent to which financial institutions must respond to those needs.

Direct Pressure. Civic groups may, as in the above example, withdraw funds from banks and register complaints with government agencies. Community leaders may demand meetings with the bank's management to insist on different treatment. Lawsuits may be filed by employees who allege that discrimination has been practiced. Picket lines, led by activists who object to a bank's practices, may appear. Each of these actions detracts from the institution's image and ultimately has its effect on the balance sheet.

A further dilemma confronts the banks in the area of social responsi-

[23]Donald T. Savage, "CRA and Community Credit Needs," *The Bankers Magazine*, January 1979, p. 51.

[24]Steven Pastore, "Redlining—or Red Herring," *The Bankers Magazine*, January 1979, p. 43.

[25]Pastore, *op. cit.*, p. 43.

[26]"Community Reinvestment Act: Questions and Answers," Federal Reserve Bank of New York, Circular 8502, January 23, 1979, and 8535, March 13, 1979.

bility in that a local population may join with labor unions and civic leaders in expecting banks to provide direct financial aid in a time of crisis. Such aid usually takes the form of purchases of the community's debt issues. This raises a question about the degree of risk that a bank can reasonably be expected to assume. It is a common belief that banks have large sums of money, consisting chiefly of their own funds, to lend and invest at will. Nothing could be further from the truth. Banks have repeatedly tried to make the point that loans and investments are made chiefly with depositors' funds rather than with the institutions' own capital. Responsibility to those depositors for the safety of their funds, and prudence in lending and investing, must be paramount in every bank's operating philosophy. A critical problem that must be addressed by contemporary bank management is inherent in this aspect of social responsibility and civic commitment.

The basic policy decision that must be made is a response to the question of whether normal criteria are to be applied when a bank is considering loans to small, minority-owned businesses, home mortgages in deteriorating areas of a city, or municipal bonds or notes as investments. To relax these criteria may be tantamount to assuming risks that would otherwise be unacceptable, thereby placing deposited funds in jeopardy and possibly incurring criticism from federal or state examiners. There have also been instances of adverse public reaction when banks followed their normal procedures and sought repayment of debt issues from municipalities that were in financial difficulty.

Voluntary Commitments. A nationwide survey conducted in 1972 disclosed that 42 percent of the respondents were "not sure" what contributions commercial banks were making to the well-being of their communities.[27] This study and others that indicated a similar lack of public appreciation of the banks' efforts led to a series of attempts to convey the opposite message. In some cases these efforts were undertaken by individual banks, as when Citibank, N.A., in New York publicized its fund that was created to purchase bullet-proof vests for police officers. In others the American Bankers Association took the initiative. This organization has recently published a detailed list of purely voluntary measures, taken by banks throughout the country, to respond to

[27] Louis Harris, *The Second Study: The American Public's and Public Opinion Leaders' Views of Banks and Bankers*, Philadelphia, The Foundation for Full Service Banks, 1972, p. 74.

particular community needs.[28] These embrace such projects as providing special facilities for the handicapped, contributing to public educational television, and donating bank officers' services to assist minority banks and businesses.

The Social Audit

Because socially responsible actions have become such an important part of the overall operations of banks and businesses, attempts have been made to quantify the extent to which these organizations have actually discharged their obligations. These efforts at performance measurement have been given the name "social audits." They are specifically designed to show the sensitivity with which a business has adapted to social change:

> The evolving means by which the corporation and others have striven to appraise the impact of its actions on society, and the manner in which it has discharged its social responsibility, have generally been described as a *social audit*.[29]

The social audit may be designed to show the expectations of social groups as identified by the bank or business, a statement of the organization's priorities in addressing these, a description of the activities that will be undertaken, and an updated report of accomplishments versus goals. Five audits of this type have been reported by nationally known firms, two of which were among the nation's largest commercial banks.[30] Several major corporations have established special committees within their boards of directors to supply input to and review the social audit; to ensure objectivity and enhance credibility, members of the board from outside the organization are usually appointed to such committees.[31] They have in effect made the social and civic contributions of the organization a part of the overall balance sheet, and their work reflects

[28]American Bankers Association, *Bankers and Community Involvement*, Washington, DC, 1978.
[29]John J. Corson and George A. Steiner, *Measuring Business's Social Performance: The Corporate Social Audit*, New York, Committee for Economic Development, 1974, p. 23. Reprinted by permission.
[30]Corson and Steiner, *op. cit.*, p. 23. The concept has also been addressed by Neil H. Jacoby in *Corporate Power and Social Responsibility*, New York, Macmillan, 1973, p. xvii.
[31]Corson and Steiner, *op. cit.*, p. 62.

the viewpoint that a business enterprise today must take account of its responsibilities as a corporate citizen even when these affect profits.[32]

COMMUNICATIONS

One final obligation of each commercial bank crosses all the boundaries that separate its various constituencies and directly affects every group with which the bank is involved. It is the obligation to communicate effectively, in every sense of the word.

Oral and written communications of every type fill the business day and have a direct bearing on the way in which the organization functions. They connect human beings to one another, forming a foundation and a bridge upon which the bank is built.[33]

Each day, members of the bank's management team must direct the staff, advertise to the public, deal with various groups representing the community, and interact with depositors. Every staff meeting within the bank, every call on or exchange of correspondence with a customer, every internal memorandum announcing procedural changes or matters affecting the staff, and every conversation between manager and subordinate can be an example of effective or ineffective transmission of desired information. The need for clear communication, whether internal or external, oral or written, has never been greater.

The autocratic manager of the past felt little need to comprehend the principles of effective communication, since his message was authoritarian, terse, and nonnegotiable. Similarly the bank's communications with its shareholders, depositors, and community were brief and impersonal. Advertising was kept to a minimum; information about the bank's basic policies was not widely disseminated; and the role of a bank in its community was taken for granted. Today, a bank's enlightened self-interest demands that all possible steps be taken to encourage and enhance communication in every direction.

Whenever stockholders have been led to understand why certain policies were adopted; whenever depositors have been told why specific actions affecting them are being taken; whenever staff members have

[32]Rockefeller, *Creative Management in Banking*, New York, McGraw-Hill, 1964, pp. 22–23.
[33]Raymond V. Lesikar, *Business Communication: Theory and Application*, rev. ed., Homewood, IL, Richard D. Irwin, 1972, pp. 3–4.

been made to feel that their suggestions are welcomed; and whenever community groups have been enlightened as to the direct contributions of the bank to civic well-being, there is a direct and positive effect on both the image of the bank and its internal efficiency. Conversely, if any constituent group is kept in the dark, and if the bank's management conveys the impression that it has no real interest in *listening*, the organization is bound to suffer. Table 2-1 provides some concrete examples of positive and negative communication that are of concern to the bank.

Table 2-1 Examples of Communication

Effective Communication	Ineffective Communication	Noncommunication
Supervisor and subordinate jointly agree on all the terms of an annual business plan and budget	A staff memorandum is unclear and filled with jargon; employees throw it away without understanding it	Subordinates cannot discuss job-related problems with superiors
A file memorandum provides complete documentation of discussions with a customer regarding a proposed loan	A clerk fails to realize the importance of each step in a job procedure	An important telephone message is not given to the right party
Employee publications clearly spell out all details of each benefit plan	A depositor is confused about the calculation of interest on a loan or account	A clerk is never told about the bank's policy on absenteeism
An annual performance review gives a full, quantitative picture of an officer's progress versus goals	A supervisor is unsure about the limits of his or her authority in the position	Employees are not told in advance of changes affecting them
The bank's annual report states and explains policies regarding involvement in, and loans to, certain nations	Publications and press releases are vague or are slanted so that only one view is presented	No effort is made to publicize the bank's socially responsible acts

III

EFFECTIVE MANAGEMENT

If it occasionally happens that members of today's bank management teams look back over their shoulders and wistfully talk of the "good old days," one can understand their nostalgic wish by recalling the many years during which commercial banking in America was a relatively static industry. The resistance to change that has been identified as a common human trait was prevalent in the banking industry. Banks offered a very limited range of services to a very limited market and encountered very little competition. The main task of management was to put to profitable use the demand deposits that steadily flowed into most of the institutions. The status quo produced adequate annual profits and did not appear to require new techniques or approaches. Attempts to visualize the future and prepare ways of coping with the changes it might bring were not considered worth the effort and expense.

To the contemporary observer it may be difficult to imagine a banking industry that made such minimal efforts to develop new services, market existing ones, or recognize the potential value of the consumer as a bank customer. Yet the industry followed that course, and it was only in the years following World War II that basic yet drastic revisions in banking philosophy began to occur.

In marked contrast to the past, banking today is an affirmation of Parmenides' axiom that "everything is change." New services are being offered to newly identified markets in new areas of the globe. New technology is simultaneously making additional services possible and changing the bank's internal operating procedures. New regulations from federal and state authorities affect commercial banks, sometimes allowing them to innovate in serving customers and on other occasions inhibiting their ability to compete. New problems in human resources management crop up as the work itself changes and as new skills are required for the "Full Service" bank. Some observers, as they notice the dynamics of change in banking, are led to state that the 1970s have witnessed more upheavals, quantitatively and qualitatively, than did the entire 14 previous decades of our banking history.[1] There is no reason to expect that the size and scope of these changes will diminish in the future. The specifics and the timing are unknown, but further changes in technology, regulation, competition, and external conditions (e.g., the money market) can most assuredly be predicted to occur.[2]

The luxury of traditionalism is one that today's bankers cannot afford unless they are prepared to face a still greater decrease in their relative position versus their competitors. Effective management today mandates that they assume a position far different from that which so many of them adopted in the past, when they simply permitted the future to happen and made no attempt to anticipate it or react to those events that might be foreseen.[3] In addition, they must discard their former parochialism, which often seemed to preclude their accepting individuals with skills or backgrounds in nonbanking disciplines or areas, or prevent their applying the management techniques that had succeeded in other industries.

One of the ironies prevalent in past management attitudes in commercial banking, for example, lies in the fact that bankers expected far more from their customers than they were prepared to implement in their own organizations. A corporate borrower was expected to be able to forecast sales and cash flow and to demonstrate an ability to plan for and adjust to change. That borrower certainly would have to be well aware of past, existing, and projected profit margins. Yet the bank that imposed those criteria probably did nothing comparable itself, nor was it

[1] Herbert V. Prochnow and Herbert V. Prochnow, Jr. (Eds.), *The Changing World of Banking*, New York, Harper & Row, 1974, p. 322.

[2] Thomas W. Thompson, Leonard L. Berry, and Philip H. Davidson, *Banking Tomorrow: Managing Markets Through Planning*, New York, Van Nostrand Reinhold, 1978, p. 18.

[3] John M. Mason, *Financial Management of Commercial Banks*, Boston, Warren, Gorham & Lamont, 1979, p. 110.

able to display the same management ability it demanded from the user of its services.

If bankers today are in fact willing to learn from others, they can give proper weight and credence to one survey of 280 chief executives, which showed that two-thirds of them considered *planning* to be their most important single activity and that they spent 44 percent of their time on it.[4] Planning is considered an absolute necessity in today's management environment. The direct costs of failure to plan may include neglect of markets, loss of market share, inability to take advantage of external developments, and wide swings in annual earnings.[5] Planning is the management technique that looks at an organization as it now stands, attempts to predict the external and internal factors that may affect it in the future, and leads to coordinated and comprehensive decision making, committing resources to certain courses of action. These courses of action are designed to help the organization attain its stated and desired objectives. Planning should occur before any other managerial functions, because it will decide the scope and nature of those functions.[6]

THE PLANNING PROCESS DEFINED

In its most simplistic form, the planning process is one that could be followed by an individual who is thinking about his or her career, a manufacturer or supplier of merchandise, or a person contemplating an automobile trip. It poses three basic questions:

Where are we now?

Where do we want to be?

How shall we get there?

Each of these three questions leads in turn to further questions that go into considerable detail. "Where are we now?," for example, is a fundamental query that leads to such questions as:

[4]John W. Humble, *How to Manage by Objectives*, New York, AMACOM, A Division of American Management Associations, 1972, p. 45.
[5]Thompson et al., *op. cit.*, p. 36.
[6]Robert M. Fulmer, *The New Management*, 2nd ed., New York, Macmillan, 1978, p. 94.

What is the nature of our business?

Which wants and needs, as we perceive them in our customers and prospective markets, are we attempting to meet?

Are there legal constraints on our doing so?

Peter Drucker[7] has specifically identified the asking of "Where are we now?" and the resulting course of action, or failure to act, as a cause for the success or bankruptcy of particular corporations.

Similarly, the question "Where do we want to be?" provokes many secondary and corollary inquiries, which may include:

What are the specific objectives of the organization?

What rate of growth does it wish to attain?

Will it endeavor to be all things to all people?

The last question is especially relevant for a bank, which must decide which components of the marketplace, and which products and services, can be utilized to help the institution reach its objectives.

To ask "How shall we get there?" is tantamount to questioning the appropriate strategies and means that flow from the answers to the first two fundamental questions. When management has determined the targets it should aim for, methods must be developed. It is impossible to divorce planning from managing. The effective managers, particularly in banks, are those who have given thought to what the future will be like, who create scenarios based on their expectations of the future, and who believe that that future can be improved for their institutions through their own decisions and actions. Bank managers today are expected to be able to make short-term decisions that contribute to the organization's long-range programs.[8]

Without a planning process, bank management may never give sufficient thought to the weaknesses and strengths of the organization as it now exists. Without a planning process, management does not make a

[7]Peter F. Drucker, *The Practice of Management*, New York, Harper & Row, 1954, p. 50.
[8]Mason, *op. cit.*, p. 110.

real determination of what the bank should be as opposed to what it is now. Without a planning process, it becomes easy for management to fall into the pattern of simply responding to crises—which means failing to act until disaster is imminent.

When planning takes place, however, a bank places itself in a position to gain a competitive advantage in one or more areas, and its management knows what must be done in order to make this happen. If a bank feels that state laws will be revised so that branching will become more possible or more extensive, it will act in advance by identifying the key locations for expansion and taking preliminary steps toward establishing its presence in these locations. If the bank believes that federal legislation may be revised so that underwriting revenue bonds is again allowed for commercial banks, it will have the personnel and systems in place ahead of time. If the bank's market research unit identifies significant demographic changes in its customer base, the institution can reshape its policies and become a leader in providing services aimed at specific market segments.

Planning, then, directly influences the image of the bank as it is perceived in the marketplace and affects the bottom line by determining what steps need be taken to maximize profits. It is also a management vehicle for communication, since it conveys the fact that the bank has a definite sense of direction and that the performance of staff members should always focus on that direction.

THE PLANNING PROCESS IMPLEMENTED

In order to implement the planning process, management must first make a specific *commitment* to it. This step must take place at the highest level of management. The Chief Executive Officer establishes the pattern. He or she must make it absolutely clear to the staff that the process is necessary, that it will lead to specific benefits, that it has the complete support of senior management, that it is not merely a paper or "make work" exercise giving lip service to the concept, that the results of the process will be closely monitored, and that one effect of the process will be the measuring of individuals' contributions to the fulfillment of the organization's stated objectives.

Given this top-level commitment, the committee or group responsible for implementing the process can then review those factors, both external and internal, that affect the bank now and will affect it in the future. The following list makes no attempt to be inclusive, but suggests some of the most probable topics:

1. *Social and economic conditions.* The projected inflation rate, predicted government reactions to that rate, projections of consumer income, interest rate assumptions, social responsibility concerns, and consumer and activist movements.
2. *Government policies and legislation.* Changes in or elimination of Regulation Q, new regulations on electronic funds transfer systems (EFTS) terminals and negotiable order for withdrawal (NOW) accounts, Federal Reserve restraints on holding company expansion or foreign branch and funding operations, and congressional action to permit revenue bond underwriting or interstate branch banking.
3. *Financial considerations.*Capital constraints, liquidity problems, tax status, existing and proposed components of bank income, ability to allocate funds to specific areas, and the existing and anticipated size and "mix" of deposits.
4. *Human resources factors.* Existing and required staff, management succession, and training and development needs.
5. *Technological consideratons.* Existing versus desired capabilities, anticipated consumer reactions to forms of EFTS, systems revisions, and estimated benefits and costs.
6. *Marketing.* Identification of international, corporate, commercial, retail, institutional, and government markets on which to focus, determination of services to be emphasized for each, appraisal of extent and effectiveness of competition, and determination of type and scope of advertising campaigns and promotions.[9]

Some banks have found it helpful to arrange for in-depth analytical discussions of this type to take place in a conference center or other location away from the bank itself. In this way the brainstorming, think tank sessions can be held without distractions or interruptions.

The next step in the implementation of the total planning process entails formulating *objectives.* These are broad, long-term, nonquantitative statements that answer the basic questions, "Where do we want to be?" Examples of objectives might include:

[9]A more comprehensive description of the analytical process may be found in Thompson, et al., *op. cit.*, pp. 51-60 and in Prochnow and Prochnow, *op. cit.*, pp. 263-264.

1. To enhance the bank's reputation as innovative and responsive to the needs and wants of its markets.
2. To improve the quality of the loan portfolio.
3. To surpass other local banks in annual growth in per-share earnings.

Objectives, in turn, lead to *goals*, which are more specific and quantitative and are usually to be attained within a shorter time. Objectives usually apply to the entire organizaiton, whereas goals generally identify particular areas where certain measurable progress is sought. Examples of goals might include:

1. Stated percentages of improvement in return on assets, return on equity, and earnings per share over the next 5 years.
2. Increases in identified segments of markets as determined by specific market share percentages.
3. Reductions in critical expense areas.

Goals should be ambitious but attainable and should contribute directly to stated objectives. They must take into account the strengths and weaknesses of the bank as identified through the analytical process. If goals require a commitment of money and equipment, management must be prepared to make a commitment for supplying the necessary resources.

Participatory management has a high priority in this process. Individuals must be made to feel free to speak frankly about existing problems of any type. Senior management must create the climate for this. If the planning process is designed merely to have the key executives tell the bank's most senior officers only what they want to hear, and if individuals are afraid to pinpoint weaknesses in the organization known to them or perceived by the market, it is actually no process at all. At some of the larger banks, this problem has been addressed through the formation of task forces, composed of groups of officers who have been given specific responsibility for positioning the institutions for the future and whose recommendations go directly to the most senior level of management.

Policies

The next step in the planning process requires formulating *policies*. These are official statements of the bank, supportive of goals and objectives, drawn up to provide guidelines for performance and to spell out the "rules of the road" for managers to follow. Policies may be of a nature that reflects the overall philosophy of the institution, such as the following:

1. Members of the bank's staff shall neither solicit nor accept fees, gifts, lavish entertainment, or other benefits intended to influence their business transactions with customers.
2. Material inside information shall never be used by the bank, its officers, or its employees in selling, buying, or recommending to others certain securities.
3. The bank shall not attempt to obtain any form of agreement from a customer that the bank's purchase of his products or services will be tied to the amount of business he gives to the bank.

In other instances, policies may be prepared and disseminated in direct consequence of the agreed-upon goals. These are concrete, rather than philosophical or ethical. Examples might include:

1. To improve our competitive position and gain a larger share of the retail market, we shall expand our installment and mortgage loan activities.
2. To achieve our goals of social responsibility, we shall provide equal opportunities for employment and advancement for all, without discrimination of any kind, and shall apply the same nondiscriminatory standards to all who apply for credit.
3. To improve management controls over key areas of the bank we shall implement a system of individual profit centers, identifying all controllable income and expenses.[10]

One advantage of the brainstorming type of meeting is that it provides participants with chances to discuss contingency plans and other courses of action. In many cases, policies should be designed with provisions for rapid changes in the event of any failure. Fully participative discussion can assist in the creation of "what if" scenarios. It may also be advisable for the process to include consideration of a potential "worst case"

[10]The concept and implementation of profit center planning are discussed in Oliver G. Wood, Jr., *Commercial Banking: Practice and Policy*, New York, D. Van Nostrand, 1978, pp. 51-59.

so that any possible adverse consequences or external factors are postulated.

Many policies are predicated on outside conditions that are highly volatile. Changes in the economy or in money market conditions may force managers to move quickly in revising the original game plan. A world crisis creates the need for immediately setting a new policy in response to it. The situation in Iran in 1979 exemplifies this need. An official repudiation of its existing debts by the new Iranian government, coupled with an announcement that all Iranian deposits outside the country would be withdrawn and repatriated, brought a quick response from several major American banks that exercised their legal right of offset of deposits against loans.

Strategies

As extensions of agreed-upon policies, the bank should then prepare specific *strategies*, consonant with goals and contributing to objectives. Thus lending officers will apply certain criteria to each credit situation as a means of contributing to the objective of improving portfolio quality. Branches will develop marketing strategies to bring in new business. The installment loan and bank card units will determine what actions to take to improve their market share.

Practices

The bank's policies and strategies are reflected in the daily *practices* of all levels of management. A member of the bank's staff acts in a certain way as a means of implementing those policies and strategies. For example, a bank may establish the objective of improving its market share in the insurance industry. A quantified, specific goal is then formulated: during the coming year, new demand deposits of $______ will result from the opening of accounts by ______ insurers. The specific strategies to be employed will then be embodied in a marketing plan that details officers' call programs and identifies the services to be offered to each prospective customer in direct response to what is known about the company's situation and needs. The operations units whose production will be affected by the new activity will be alerted so that any necessary acquisitions of equipment and personnel can be planned. The entire process culminates in the practice, which is the work performed by calling officers in soliciting accounts.

Planning amounts to little more than an expensive and time consuming paper exercise unless the ongoing performance of each unit is monitored against the plan. A bank establishes certain objectives and incorporates them into annual operating plans. Every level of its management is then expected to make measurable, direct contributions to the fulfillment of the plan. Annual or semiannual performance reviews of each officer can be designed to include the specific controllable results he or she has achieved as compared with specific goals.

None of the foregoing should be construed to mean that planning is merely a mechanism by which higher levels of management impose arbitrary strategies and goals on subordinates without the benefit of input from the latter. Communication, again, is an essential part of the process. Line managers must be free to contribute their ideas and must have some degree of latitude to interpret corporate goals for their own particular circumstances and environments. Whenever it becomes necessary to revise plans, line managers should be able to document the reasons and justify the changes.

A branch manager, for example, may have agreed to certain profit and deposit goals for a particular year. However, owing to changes in the neighborhood through population shifts, or because a major company on which the branch depended for much of its activity has closed its plant, or as a result of an aggressive promotional campaign mounted by a nearby competitor, the branch's deposits may have decreased. By midyear it may become apparent that the original targets cannot be met. It would be grossly unjust to penalize the manager for this combination of external factors that are beyond his or her control. Therefore, the goals must be reviewed in the light of contributory factors.

STRUCTURING

As a result of the planning process, management may decide that the existing structure of the bank is not one that is most likely to achieve the objectives that have been set. It may be appropriate to redesign that structure so that units of the bank can focus on specific areas of the market.

Many major banks, for example, traditionally were structured with

National Divisions that handled all accounts outside their own geographic areas, while Metropolitan Divisions were responsible for all types of accounts—major corporations, smaller businesses, nonprofit organizations, and individuals—within those areas. The structuring of the organization was based entirely on geographical considerations.

This division of responsibilities has undergone major changes at several of these banks in recent years. Instead of following a geographical division, the banks are now structured according to customer type. At these institutions a so-called Corporate Bank or Corporate Banking Group is, in effect, a "wholesale" bank; it handles all phases of the bank's relationships with the largest corporate customers. This entity may be subdivided along industry lines so that teams of officers specialize in the petroleum, transporation, chemical, food, or other industry sectors. Under this type of organization, geography is entirely irrelevant. The offices of two of the corporations handled by the same banking team may be thousands of miles apart.

The banks that follow this path also create new entities within their organizations to handle the needs of smaller businesses and of consumers, who represent the market focused on through the banks' network of branches.

Creation of organizational structures with so many levels, however, would logically occur only at the larger banks. In small institutions a simpler structure would suffice. It is a basic responsibility of management to determine what divisions should exist over and above the most basic ones (Trust, Auditing, Human Resources, and the like).

The structure of the organization and the formation of profit centers within it may be viewed as a logical adjunct to the concept of management by objectives. Officers who are placed in charge of each unit should understand the roles their areas play in the overall bank and must recognize that their performance will be reviewed according to the contributions their units make to overall profitability. There should be no doubt in any individual's mind that performance on his or her part leading to goal fulfillment will lead to rewards. Job satisfaction will result from this, but will not constitute the objective; the objective is to bring an individual's goals into harmony with those of the organization and to motivate that level of personal performance that makes it possible for both to be realized.[11]

[11]Wayne B. Lewin, "Banking Productivity Versus Personal Goals," *Bank Administration*, October 1979, p. 10.

ACCOUNTABILITY

New approaches to effective management in banking often include the preparation of job descriptions for various levels of the staff. These clearly outline the importance of the job in the overall picture, the areas of responsibility that the job embraces, the required skills, the number of individuals supervised, and the position objectives. Job descriptions may then be classified according to relative points, arrived at through a synthesis of all the above factors. Levels of compensation then become direct functions of the number of points assigned to each position.

An important aspect of the job description lies in the assigning and acceptance of accountability. An officer is expected to delegate tasks; those who fail to do so are automatically poor managers because they have made no attempt to allow juniors to assume more responsibility and thus have not provided for proper management succession. Every manager's performance review should include mention of what he or she has done or failed to do in training and preparing his or her own replacement.

Delegation, however, does not absolve a manager from accountability. The end results produced must be the yardstick by which performance is evaluated. An individual cannot point to the subordinates' errors or shortcomings as an excuse for the performance of the department or branch. The concept of accountability may have first been clearly identified in professional sports; a team's manager or coach is rewarded or fired as the team succeeds or fails. More recently, the same principle has been applied to corporate and bank management at every level, including those of the Chairman and President. Outright terminations, and resignations "by mutual consent," of officers at the most senior levels of nationally known corporations and banks have become commonplace whenever their organizations displayed any type of substandard performance. An individual who is promoted to a role of greater responsibility must accept the fact that it is the bottom-line, eventual results that will decide his or her reward. If problems or weaknesses that inhibit goal attainment exist, the manager must take corrective action rather than attempt to use them in justification of his or her failure to reach a goal.

SYSTEMS AND CONTROLS

Each refinement of computer capability brings with it increased awareness of the multitude of reports that can be provided to management regarding every aspect of the bank's overall operations. As part of its ongoing effort to monitor performance versus goals, a bank may generate monthly reports showing the income and expenses for departments and branches. These may be subdivided to give detailed breakdowns under each of these two basic headings so that such factors as interest income, earnings on balances, clerical and official salaries, and the like, can be clearly seen and compared with budget projections. On a daily basis, statistical data on account balances, overdrafts, loans, and accruals can be provided. Pro forma figures can be projected over given periods of time to show the end results of decisions. The loan portfolio report can be subdivided to show industry concentrations, types of loans outstanding, delinquencies, or other meaningful data. Profit-and-loss reports can be produced for bank services. Simulation techniques can be used to assist in decision making.

However, these advances in information technology serve no real purpose unless management uses them to institute whatever controls may be necessary. If the computer reports show that a certain service has become unprofitable, that a branch is steadily losing money, or that a particular policy has worked to the detriment of the organization, management must take appropriate action.

This concept applies throughout the organization. A relationship manager to whom a group of accounts is assigned can determine whether sufficient balances are being maintained with the bank each month to support the levels of activity and services rendered. If a shortfall exists, the manager is then expected to use the information to negotiate with the customers and remedy the situation. If the management information system clearly shows that a certain department regularly fails to meet its goals, its manager must identify the reasons and correct the problem.

Computers should not be thought of as running a bank; rather, they should be considered as the tools that provide timely and relevant data, facilitating and justifying the decisions managers must make.

RESPONSIBLE UNITS

In varying degrees and to varying extents, three units are involved in the planning process. They play roles of greater or lesser magnitude in establishing objectives and goals, determining strategies, putting policies into effect, monitoring results, and making decisions resulting from that monitoring. The three units consist of the bank's *stockholders*, *directors*, and *officers*.

In smaller banks the number of stockholders may be limited to members of a single family; in the largest American banks there may be 50,000 or more. This distinction makes the degree of stockholder participation in the management process quite different in each case. At the major money center banks, the shareholder base is so large and diversified that, with the exception of a vocal minority that raises questions, criticizes, and introduces resolutions for change, the involvement is minimal. Elsewhere it is not uncommon to find that the senior officers, major stockholders, and dominant figures on the board are one and the same, and therefore these few individuals are, in effect, the bank's managers.

The extent of stockholder involvement, however, is immaterial. The important fact is that the bank's basic and ongoing obligation to them makes them a *de facto* element in all considerations of bank management. Shareholders look to the board of directors to draw up proper policies for the institution's profitability and growth and to see to it that those policies are put into practice. They want and expect their stake in the bank's future to appreciate and be protected over the course of time.

Directors, as was noted earlier, are at the apex of the organization chart and are legally responsible for supervising the bank's affairs. They are expected to know the bank's mission, define its objectives, set its policies, ensure the legality and prudence of its actions and decisions, be accountable for the results, select the managers who will implement policies, and accept personal liability (under certain circumstances) for losses the bank may sustain. For the guidance of individuals serving as directors of national banks, the Comptroller of the Currency has published a bulletin, enumerating and detailing their responsibilities and liabilities.[12] The concept of accountability is an important element in that bulletin. Directors cannot claim ignorance of what management has done, nor can they use their own absence from board meetings as an excuse.

Bank boards typically include committees, either required by law or designated in the bank's bylaws, to supervise the credit, trust, investment, and auditing functions.[13] Directors must review each report of a government agency's examination of the bank and take any necessary

[12] *Duties and Liabilities of Directors of National Banks*, Washington, DC, U.S. Government Printing Office, 1972.

[13] Howard D. Crosse and George H. Hempel, *Management Policies for Commercial Banks*, 2nd ed., Englewood Cliffs, NJ, Prentice-Hall, 1973, p. 52.

corrective action.[14] They represent all the constituencies to which the bank is obligated and, in this role, must investigate any matter within their power and order appropriate changes.[15]

National banks must have at least five, but not more than twenty-five, directors; state laws vary. Both federal and state statutes require them to own stock in the bank and prevent their serving as directors of any competing commercial bank in the same geographic area.[16]

Although both the stockholder and director groups play important roles, it is the third component, the bank's officers, to which major attention must be directed in any consideration of effective management. It is the basic role of the official staff not only to carry out the policies set by the board, but to propose new ones that may be more consistent with changing times. Officers must keep the directors informed, take advantage of their expertise, and utilize them as a court of last resort in those instances when decisions cannot be made at any lower level. Officers have a daily involvement in all the functions of the organization, and an exposure to the attitudes and needs of the marketplace, which no other group can have. Their input to higher levels of bank management and, through the latter, to the board is invaluable.

The daily actions and behavior patterns of bank officers as they explain, interpret, and implement policies should be consistent with the goals of the overall organization and a positive factor in the successes of their own units. They must review and coordinate, train and develop, establish accountability for juniors, and assure quality performance.

The last task is critical in banking, since the huge daily volume of transactions and documents creates inherent statistical probabilities of error. The costs of quality control and the methods used to achieve it can be considered an integral part of the planning process. Management must constantly look at not only the errors that leave the bank (e.g., the misposted check, the incorrect advice, or the statement sent to the wrong customer) but at those that are detected before a task is completed. The former category causes time-consuming, expensive inquiries and adjustments, hurts the bank's image, and may result in losses of accounts. The latter category requires allocating time and money to a system of superimposed layers to inspect and verify work. The errors themselves create

[14] Wood, *op. cit.*, p. 33.

[15] Edward W. Reed, Richard V. Cotter, Edward K. Gill, and Richard K. Smith, *Commercial Banking*, Englewood Cliffs, NJ, Prentice-Hall, 1976, p. 59.

[16] Martin Mayer, *The Bankers*, New York, David McKay Co., 1974, p. 64. Crosse and Hempel, *op. cit.*, p. 52, provide additional detail.

forms expense and necessitate repetition of tasks. The goals that were determined in the planning process can be frustrated by a lack of concern for the matter of quality control.

CONTROLS AND AUDITING

No discussion of the tasks and problems of bank management today would be complete without reference to the measures that must be taken to safeguard the bank's own funds and those of its customers. Minimizing risk is a critical task in the management process. Every increase in the number and dispersion of branches, the size of the staff, and the range of services brings a need for more stringent controls and auditing.

Controls are the various measures taken by the bank to prevent or reduce loss or risk. When two individuals are required to verify each other's work, or when specific procedures are established for a task, controls are in place. On the other hand, *auditing* in banking describes the ongoing effort to ensure that all necessary controls have been installed and that all required procedures are actually being followed.

Federal Bureau of Investigation reports disclose consistent annual increases in the number of bank robberies. Newspaper stories repeatedly publicize cases of improper loans or speculative foreign exchange trades, missing or stolen securities, and wire transfers that were fraudulently entered through a bank's computers.[17] American Bankers Association statistics covering a 10-year period reported an average of 177 defalcations at banks, each involving $10,000 or more.[18] As the active, governing body of the corporation, the board must accept responsibility for implementing all needed policies and systems relevant to bank security. Directors usually designate one officer to supervise the internal controls program and to conduct all internal examinations. This individual, commonly called the auditor, is appointed by the board and reports directly to it on all matters involving the safety and efficiency of operations and the accuracy and completeness of all records.

Auditors must be completely independent and have absolute control over their performance. The bank examination conducted by a state or federal agency is concerned primarily with the institution's compliance with all laws and regulations and with its true financial condition. Fed-

[17]Crosse and Hempel, *op. cit.*, p. 239.
[18]In *ibid.*, p. 241.

eral and state examiners cannot go into minute detail for every phase of a bank's operations, nor are they specifically trying to locate embezzlements or frauds. It is the bank's own auditors who must do so.

Any bank employee who has been a part of both an internal and external examination of his or her bank usually reports that the former is far more rigorous and detailed. This is exactly as it should be. The bank must police itself thoroughly; it cannot afford the luxury of waiting for a federal or state examining team to identify problems and suggest measures to improve security.

In addition to actually conducting unannounced examinations within the bank, the chief auditor may also address such questions as the security programs that are in effect in the human resources area. The auditor may check to see if fingerprints and references of job applicants are being verified or if access to personnel files is being restricted to authorized persons. He or she may also institute controls over numbered forms or documents, including debit and credit advices, and may examine all records of overdrafts and customers' drawings against uncollected funds. Auditors constantly attempt to approach the question of the bank's risk from three viewpoints: How great is the risk? Why is it being incurred? What can be done to minimize it? Bank audit programs, in short, are designed to ensure that whatever can be done for protection is actually being done.

No foolproof system to protect every aspect of a bank's operations in every branch and department has ever been devised. Regulatory officials agree that efforts to frustrate every bank security measure will continue and that new techniques and schemes will be used to do so.[19] That fact, however, should not deter management from an equal, unceasing, and thorough effort of its own through which all possible controls are installed for the protection of the bank's own assets and those entrusted to it by customers.

MANAGEMENT IN ACTION

The "management by crisis" thinking that seems to have prevailed among many banks in the past is simply unacceptable in today's envi-

[19]Curt Miller, "The . . . $1.5 Million Embezzlement Case," *Bank Systems and Equipment*, May 1973, p. 35 (Bank name deleted from title).

ronment. The former passive attitude, unreceptive to change and characterized by such expressions as "wait and see" or "we never did it that way before," must give way to a more enlightened philosophy.

Commercial banking consists essentially of generating profits by rendering services. To accomplish this twofold objective, a commitment to change is required.[20] That commitment is a necessary part of the total planning process, which, in turn, is an essential part of contemporary management in action.

The process entails a series of bench marks and principles. Management must develop and disseminate clearly defined objectives and goals. The elements in the future that will have an impact on the organization's tasks must be identified, and basic policies and strategies to meet them must be drawn up. Management must consider the bank as an entity that must change as its customers, its environment, and the economy of which it is such an important part are changing. As a result of this process, planning can create a work climate in which managers and subordinates know where the bank wants to be and are familiar with the measures that will be taken to lead it in that direction.

Effective planning makes possible a system by which members of a bank's staff know what is expected of them, know the time frame within which they should accomplish certain goals, and know the contributions that are expected of them so that the desired bottom-line results can be attained. Table 3-1 illustrates a specimen work plan in which an objective is stated and each milestone, leading toward its attainment, is identified.

Through receptivity to new ideas, flexibility in thinking, and willingness to risk mistakes (and admit and correct them when they occur), a bank's directors, stockholders, and officers are involved, in different ways and to varying extents, in the planning process. Their joint efforts can shape the course of the bank's future instead of merely perpetuating the present.[21]

[20]Mason, *op. cit.*, pp. 120-121.

[21]Douglas V. Austin and Gene S. Booker (Eds.), *Modern Techniques in Bank Management*, Boston, Warren, Gorham & Lamont, 1969, p. 14.

Table 3-1 Program summary and work plan

SEGMENT: (1) RETAIL BANKING — ATTACK PLAN: (1) EXPLORE PROFITABILITY + MARKET NEEDS

PROGRAM: (1) FEASIBILITY OF BRANCH EXPANSION — MANAGER: W.R. SMITH

SPECIFIC PROGRAM OBJECTIVE:

DETERMINE IF ADDITIONAL BRANCHES ARE 1) NECESSARY FOR MARKET
2) POTENTIALLY PROFITABLE

CRITICAL ASSUMPTIONS TO MONITOR:

1. NEIGHBORHOODS WILL REMAIN ESSENTIALLY UNCHANGED

2. CUSTOMERS WILL PREFER ACTUAL BRANCHES TO AUTOMATED FACILITIES

IS THE TIMELY EXECUTION OF THIS PROGRAM ESSENTIAL FOR MEETING THE FINANCIAL OBJECTIVES OF THE SEGMENT STRATEGY — YES [X] NO [ ]

#	PHASE ONE MILESTONE	DATE
1.	CONDUCT MARKET RESEARCH RE EXISTING COMPETITION IN AREA; SHOW EACH ON MAP	6/30
2.	IDENTIFY ANY POTENTIAL CHANGES IN AREA (NEW HOUSING, OFFICES, ETC.)	6/30
3.	COMPLETE DEMOGRAPHIC STUDY OF AREA (POPULATION, INCOME, ETC.)	8/1
4.	CONDUCT MARKET RESEARCH RE NEEDED/WANTED BANKING SERVICES IN AREA	9/15
5.	IDENTIFY BRANCH PROFIT POTENTIAL FOR FIRST THROUGH FIFTH YEARS	10/1
6.	SELECT OPTIMUM LOCATIONS ON BASIS OF ALL ABOVE FACTORS, OR JUSTIFY "NO GO"	11/1
7.	IF "GO" QUANTIFY HUMAN RESOURCES NEEDS AND	11/15
8.	INITIATE REAL ESTATE NEGOTIATIONS	

IV

SOURCES OF BANK FUNDS

An apocryphal story claims that four officers, each representing a different commercial bank, met to discuss the planning processes their respective banks had initiated. "Our biggest concern," said the first banker, "is *liquidity*. We're prepared to pay far less attention to other considerations because we know many of our customers are really worried over recent bank failures and problems. They want absolute assurance that they can withdraw their funds from us at any time. We see our main job as emphasizing that availability for them. No matter what else we may neglect, we're going to guarantee liquidity at all times."

"That's all well and good," said the second, "but in our case we're much more conscious of the need for *safety*. Our customers have heard one scare story after another about all the bad loans that banks have made in the past few years and how much they've had to charge off. Liquidity can take second place in our thinking. We're focusing on risk and we're determined to let the world know how prudent and conservative we've become. We simply refuse to take the risks we took last year or the year before. Besides, how in the world can your bank build up liquidity to that extent? What do you plan on doing? Will you fill up every inch of space in every vault with currency?"

"You're both on the wrong track," said the third bank officer. "We're in business purely and simply to make money. Everything else must be secondary. *Income* is the key ingredient in our game plan. Stockholders, investment analysts, newspapers, and everyone else—they look at our bottom line. They all know our bank has had some substandard earnings the past few years, and it makes no sense for us to worry about anything else until we improve our image by increasing our net income. This year you'll see the difference. It's no secret: our emphasis is on a very ambitious profit plan, because *that's* the real name of the game today."

Like the three blind men in the fable who tried to describe an elephant, each of the three bank officers was partially correct, yet each was unable to see the complete picture. It was only the fourth officer who was able to put the entire problem into the proper perspective.

"All three of you have lost sight of one of the basics of today's bank management," he said. "Of course you're right when you say that no bank can neglect considerations of liquidity and safety, and of course you're correct when you say that income is tremendously important. But whenever you overemphasize any of those three elements at the expense of the other two, you're doing nothing but creating problems for yourselves. If you can't manage your bank's funds by balancing all three objectives, you've lost the battle."

His comments summarize one of the most vital issues facing the bank management team today. The banker is no longer an *asset* manager, whose work consists chiefly of putting to profitable use the funds that automatically and regularly flow into his bank on an interest-free basis. Today's banker must be a *liability* manager. Generally speaking, banks today find that they must *buy* whatever funds they need. Only then can they use the funds in a way that combines the principles of *liquidity*, *safety*, and *income*.

The banker, then, has come to resemble a manufacturer who had somehow been able to obtain the necessary raw materials for his business at no cost but suddenly found that he had to begin paying a high price for them. The unpleasant but inescapable fact is that demand deposits no longer flow into, build up in, and remain with the commercial banks as they once did. Banks must recognize that they can no longer count on demand deposits to fund their loans and investments. Since the early 1960s, the most dramatic shift in our entire banking history has taken place in the "mix" of our deposits. In 1950, demand deposits constituted 74 percent of commercial bank deposits; by 1974, they made up only 43 percent.[1] The change in ratio continues. As of October 1979 demand

[1] Edward W. Reed, Richard V. Cotter, Edward K. Gill, and Richard K. Smith, *Commercial Banking*, Englewood Cliffs, NJ, Prentice-Hall, 1976, p. 84.

deposits accounted for only 37 percent of all deposits in the commercial banking system.[2] These cost-free deposits are no longer the bank's basic stock-in-trade; savings and time deposits dominate the scene and bring with them problems in the management of funds that prior generations of bankers never had to face.

This evolutionary trend causes the banks to pose new and challenging questions about their business. They must identify the sources of funds on which they now depend and know the costs of these funds in a highly competitive marketplace. They must offset these costs through their loan and investment policies and practices. Their profit planning must reflect the new structure of their deposit base.

HISTORICAL DEVELOPMENT

Prior to the Depression of 1930 and 1931, commercial banks in America were allowed to pay interest on demand deposits, and many of the major institutions in money market centers aggressively vied with one another for new business by offering attractive interest rates to their corporate, institutional, and government customers and prospects. In periods of economic prosperity and increasing competition, the rates offered as a means of attracting accounts rose accordingly. However, to meet the expense created by rising interest costs, banks in many cases had to make some sacrifice of loan portfolio quality. Safety became less important than income. By accepting higher-risk loans, the banks could charge higher interest rates and thus offset their increased costs.

Loans of substandard quality were a causative factor in the collapse of many banks during the early 1930s.[3] Those failures, numbering in the thousands and causing losses of billions of dollars, were taken into account by Congress when legislation calling for the reform of the banking system was being considered in 1933. That legislation, as enacted in its final form, contained several restrictive features, one of which prohibited all payment of interest on demand deposits.

The Banking Act of 1935 expanded on this by giving the Federal Reserve the power to establish maximum interest rates on various forms of savings and time deposits at member banks. Under this Act, Regulation Q of the Federal Reserve came into being. It remains operative

[2] *Federal Reserve Bulletin*, November 1979, p. A16.
[3] Paul S. Nadler, *Commercial Banking in the Economy*, New York, Random House, 1968, p. 61.

today as a critical and, more recently, a highly controversial element in controlling the interest rate structure.

As long as the commercial banking system was able to maintain an ample reservoir of interest-free demand deposits and put those funds to use in loans and investments, bankers were asset managers in a business that may be described as "funds-using."[4] Whenever loan demand from preferred customers increased, banks simply sold portions of their holdings of government bonds and used the proceeds to fund the loans. There was always an adequate supply of available money to meet the bank's needs.

However, in the years following World War II, the commercial banks as a group began losing ground relative to other financial intermediaries. Affluent individuals and sophisticated financial officers in corporations, government agencies, and institutions, started to recognize the many opportunities that had opened up for them. Increasingly, they found that there were many ways of putting their funds to work at a profit instead of leaving those funds in a noninterest-bearing checking account.

Savings banks and savings and loan associations frequently use the term "disintermediation" to describe the volatility of their deposits and the fact that funds flow away from their institutions in large amounts whenever higher-yielding opportunities are available. In the postwar years, commercial banks could have used the same term to describe their outflows of funds. The basic difference lies in the fact that deposits were withdrawn from commercial banks and deposited in the thrift institutions, whereas today deposits are withdrawn from the thrifts to be placed in nonbank media, such as government obligations or investment funds.

Although disintermediation is indeed a problem for the thrifts, the fact remains that in the postwar years they achieved remarkable growth relative to that of the commercial banks. From 1946 to 1956, total deposits at all insured commercial banks increased 38 percent; during the same period, deposits at mutual savings banks and savings and loan associations increased 172 percent.[5]

[4]Howard D. Crosse and George H. Hempel, *Management Policies for Commercial Banks*, 2nd ed., Englewood Cliffs, NJ, Prentice-Hall, 1973, p. 109.

[5]Carl T. Arlt, "The Changing Character of Bank Deposits", in Herbert V. Prochnow and Herbert V. Prochnow, Jr. (Eds.), *The Changing World of Banking*, New York, Harper & Row, 1974, p. 59.

Perhaps the most significant characteristic of the commercial banks' approach to this situation was the slowness with which they recognized their relative decline in the marketplace and attempted to respond. For many years, while their competitors were steadily attracting deposits at their expense, the commercial banks insisted on maintaining their traditional postures, disdaining the consumer as a customer, and neglecting any major marketing effort. Most commercial bank officers seem to have felt that customers and prospects knew of the bank and knew where it was, and would approach it if necessary. No attempt was made to encroach on the savings account field, since that was viewed as the exclusive province of thrift institutions. The commercial banks saw themselves as corporate-oriented holders of demand deposits and, despite the statistics, appear to have assumed that they would always remain in a preferential, funds-using position.

Commercial banks, as a group, were also by far the largest holders of government obligations. At the end of World War II, they held almost 60 percent of their total assets in this medium, and this represented over one-third of the total national debt.[6] By law, the "Fed" was required to buy back at par value any such obligations from the banks at any time. Hence any holdings of government bonds could, without difficulty, immediately be converted into usable funds at fixed prices. The inflationary cycle that the nation experienced in the early stages of the Korean War (1950 and 1951) resulted in the abolition of existing laws on this subject.

The Accord of March 4, 1951 between the Federal Reserve and the Treasury Department gave the Fed complete freedom in its open market purchases and sales of government obligations and eliminated the concept of fixed-price support. Government bonds therefore were trading freely. As the government found it necessary to pay higher interest rates to attract funds, further disintermediation from the commercial banking system took place at the same time that credit demands were rapidly increasing. These two factors combined to create steadily rising ratios of loans to deposits at commercial banks.[7]

The savings and loan associations, as a group, displayed the greatest increases in growth relative to that of the commercial banking system. In 1946, total commercial bank deposits were $144 billion, while the

[6]Martin Mayer, *The Bankers*, New York, David McKay Co., 1974, p. 187.
[7]Nadler, *op. cit.*, p. 153.

savings and loans held $8 billion. During the ensuing 25 years the former had grown to $543 billion, increasing 3.76 times, while the latter grew to $175 billion, increasing 21.8 times.[8] By attracting new deposits the savings and loan associations were able to assume the dominant role that they still hold in the financing of home mortgages.

Commercial banks found their competition growing in type as well as in asset size. From 1945 to 1960 the total assets of life insurance companies tripled and those of trusteed pension funds increased fifteen times.[9] Corporate treasurers were prohibited by law from opening savings accounts at member banks with corporate funds,[10] but could readily select from many other investment media, providing them with interest income on what had theretofore been sterile funds in commercial bank checking accounts. Even more latitude existed for individuals. They could easily move funds from checking accounts to thrift institutions or invest in federal or municipal obligations at very attractive yields. Those with larger amounts of cash available could generate income through bankers' acceptances or prime commercial paper. The decade of the 1950s showed an 80 percent growth in America's gross national product (GNP), but only a 21 percent increase in demand deposits at commercial banks.[11]

Eventually the Federal Reserve responded to the twin pressures on commercial banks (i.e., slow growth of demand deposits while credit demands were increasing) by revising Regulation Q so that higher interest rates could be paid on savings and time deposits. The Fed also restructured its reserve requirements for member banks, encouraging them to compete for such deposits with thrift institutions. Today, required reserves on savings and time deposits are approximately one-fourth those on demand deposits.

Further complicating the problem of attracting and retaining funds was the postwar rise to prominence of the credit unions. These organizations were originally confined to use by employees of a single company or unit of government. Today, it is legally possible for any group of individuals having some common characteristic or purpose to obtain a

[8] Carter H. Golembe, "The Organization of Modern Banking," in Prochnow and Prochnow, *op. cit.*, p. 14.

[9] Mayer, *op. cit.*, p. 190.

[10] Federal Reserve regulations were revised in 1975 so that this restriction was eliminated. Corporate savings accounts up to $150,000 are now permitted.

[11] Nadler, *op. cit.*, p. 158.

charter and form a credit union. Once established, this type of financial institution can offer a wide range of services directly affecting the commercial banking system. In addition to their traditional functions of attracting members' deposits and making loans to them at preferential rates, credit unions now provide check-like instruments, known as "share drafts," for bill paying[12] and are entering the home mortgage and credit card fields.

In 1950 total deposits at credit unions were a modest $1 billion. By 1960 they had reached $5 billion and by 1974, $26 billion.[13] At year-end 1978 there were 22,272 such unions, with total deposits of over $62 billion.[14] Commercial bankers must necessarily ask how much of these deposits might have been placed with them had it not been for the credit unions' aggressive competition.

THE CERTIFICATE OF DEPOSIT

In 1961 the then First National City Bank of New York (now Citibank, N.A.) introduced a revolutionary new type of money market instrument, the *negotiable certificate of deposit*, in direct response to the need for attracting new funds. The C/D, as it has commonly become known, must be granted a permanent position of prominence among the major developments in the American banking system. Its growth has been remarkable. From a zero base in 1960, C/Ds attained a nationwide figure of over $12 billion in 1964 and over $72 billion in 1974.[15] By October 1979, those commercial banks with assets of $750 million or more reported negotiable C/Ds of over $90.6 billion,[16] and this is by no means an all-inclusive figure. It does not reflect any C/D activity at smaller banks, nor does it include any C/Ds issued for less than $100,000.

[12]In May 1979 the District of Columbia Court of Appeals declared this function illegal. The case is under appeal at this time.

[13]Reed et al., *op. cit.*, p. 86.

[14]*American Banker*, May 17, 1979, p. 3.

[15]M. A. Schapiro & Co., Inc., "The Changing Deposit Structure," *Bank Stock Quarterly*, New York, May 1974, p. 2.

[16]*Federal Reserve Bulletin*, November 1979, p. A23.

In addition to their attractiveness in terms of interest rates (Federal Reserve regulations do not apply to C/Ds for $100,000 or more; hence the rate a bank is willing to pay is a matter of competitive policy alone), their FDIC protection within standard insurance limits, and their status as direct, guaranteed obligations of banks, these certificates offered investors an important advantage that previous instruments had lacked: they were issued in negotiable form. The holder of this type of C/D could readily sell it in the secondary market at any time.

Introduction of the negotiable C/D undoubtedly enabled commercial banks to attract funds that otherwise would have been placed with competitive financial intermediaries. Indeed, the statement has been made, perhaps oversimplistically, that were it not for the C/D, commercial banking might display no deposit growth at all.[17] However, it must be regarded as somewhat of a mixed blessing. It is largely responsible for the fact that interest paid to depositors has become the largest, fastest-growing, and least controllable item of bank expense. The typical large commercial bank today finds that its direct interest expense far exceeds salaries and wages, taxes, or other costs of doing business. In 1951, when the average rate paid on all savings and time deposits at commercial banks was 1.03 percent, interest paid to depositors was 14 percent of total bank operating expenses; by 1973 the average rate had risen to 5.98 percent, and interest expense accounted for 45 percent of total operating expenses.[18] As a liability manager, the commercial banker today is a buyer of funds in a highly competitive marketplace. A new breed of customer has appeared: the shopper who has realized the value of his or her funds to the banks and who goes from one to another, seeking the highest rate. Any bank that wishes to curtail its growth in annual interest expense can do so only by lessening its competitive posture in the C/D area.

Table 4-1 graphically displays the changes in the deposit structure at all insured commercial banks in selected years from 1960 to 1978. It illustrates the point that banking today is oriented toward time, rather than demand, deposits—a complete departure from tradition.

MONEY MARKET CERTIFICATES

The trend toward various forms of time deposits received further strong impetus when the various federal regulatory authorities—the Federal

[17]Nadler, *op. cit.*, p. 164.
[18]Reed et al., *op. cit.*, p. 428.

Table 4-1 Deposit structure of all insured commercial banks for selected years, 1960–1978 (in $ millions)[a]

	1960	1965	1970	1975	1978
Total deposits in domestic offices	229	332	483	781	1016
Demand	156	183	247	321	400
Time	73	148	235	459	616

Source. Federal Deposit Insurance Corporation.
[a]Totals may not add due to rounding.

Reseve, FDIC, and Federal Home Loan Bank Board—issued new regulations in 1978, authorizing the institutions under their respective jurisdictions to offer a new form of instrument called the money market certificate (MMC).

The regulations specified that MMCs were to be issued for periods of exactly 26 weeks and that the minimum denomination would be $10,000. The ceiling rate for commercial banks was established at the discount rate for the most recently issued 6-month Treasury bills.

When the first money market certificates were offered to the public in June 1978, compounding of interest was permitted, and mutual savings banks and savings and loan associations were allowed to pay interest at a rate ¼ percent higher than the commercial bank rate. On March 15, 1979, by further action of the Federal Reserve, FDIC, and Federal Home Loan Bank Board, interest compounding was prohibited at all financial institutions, and the interest rate differential was eliminated whenever the Treasury bill rate was 9 percent or more.

The growth of MMCs within a very short period parallels that of the negotiable C/D. As of July 25, 1979 over $62 billion was outstanding in this form of deposit. A form of internal disintermediation took place at commercial banks and, to a greater extent, at thrift institutions as customers moved their funds into this higher-yielding medium. In the third quarter of 1979, net issuance of MMCs at commercial banks was $17 billion. Elimination of the interest rate differential between them and their thrift competitors resulted in the fact that more than one-half of the net issuance took place at the commercial banks.[19]

[19]*Federal Reserve Bulletin*, October 1979, p. 881.

The ever-increasing importance of the time and savings deposit function, with its accompanying rise in interest expense, has forced major revisions in bank profit planning and has helped to bring about a more widespread recognition that the term "profit margin" can be applied to banking as well as it can to any other industry. The spread at any time between the cost of funds to a bank, and the yield it derives from loaning or investing them, has become one of the most significant factors affecting the bottom line of bank performance.

A banker today, unlike his or her predecessor, is necessarily a liability manager, usually dealing in purchased funds. Decisions must be made, often during one day, as to whether the quoted rate for negotiable C/Ds and other forms of time deposits should be raised or lowered. The *quid pro quo* that determines the bank selected by a depositor is often the current interest rate on time deposits. During the first 4 months of 1979, one major commercial bank in New York City changed its quoted rates on negotiable C/Ds on an average of six times per month. Interest rates, as seen in the fact that the prime reached an unheard-of high of twenty percent in Spring 1980, necessarily rose on loans. As Treasury bill and commercial paper rates escalated, the banks found it necessary to revise their lending policies. Those types of loans on which maximum interest rates were restricted by law became far more difficult for the borrower to obtain. In this respect, thrift institutions experienced even more severe blows to their profit margin than did commercial banks. For savings and loan associations and mutual savings banks, the mortgage loan area—their primary vehicle for profitable use of funds—became a drain on earnings, since the institutions were borrowing on a short-term basis (through the MMC instrument, in many cases) at high interest rates in order to fund long-term mortgages at lesser yields.

OBJECTIVES OF FUNDS MANAGEMENT

The fundamental change in deposit structure that has taken place in the commercial banking system serves only to heighten the pressure to achieve that critical balance among the three objectives of funds management—liquidity, safety, and income—that is necessary if the bank is to meet all its obligations to all its constituents. The fourth banker in the story told at the beginning of this chapter recognized that any type of overemphasis on one objective at the expense of the other two would render a gross disservice to the entire bank. It is appropriate here to explore this in more detail.

Liquidity

Liquidity for a bank describes the institution's ability to meet customer demands for the withdrawal or payment of funds. Liquidity is obviously essential. Any refusal by a bank to honor such a demand at any time can start a run on that bank and trigger a financial crisis.

Yet no bank considers it realistic to expect all its customers to issue checks at the same time for the sum total of their demand deposit balances. Similarly not all passbook customers will withdraw their entire savings account balances, or present all their various forms of time deposit instruments for redemption, on the same day. Total liquidity would require that the bank be prepared to meet just such an eventuality, but practical considerations dictate otherwise. If a bank were to try to meet this ultimate goal, it would be forced to keep its vaults overflowing with currency, its balances with correspondents at absurdly high levels, and its noninterest-bearing reserves at the Fed in amounts far beyond the requirements. These three are its *primary* reserves. They represent cash or its immediate equivalent and are the principal source of bank liquidity. They produce no income.[20]

Secondary reserves are less liquid, but have the advantage of making a contribution to liquidity while generating income. There is a slightly higher degree of risk attached to them. The most common examples of secondary reserves include short-term government issues, bankers' acceptances, and other high-quality noncash assets that can be sold immediately if necessary.

The funds management effort frequently takes the form of a projection of the bank's "floor" of deposits and its "ceiling" for loans. Using all the available data, the bank tries to estimate how far the deposits can be expected to decrease from their current base and how greatly loan demand will probably increase over the same period. Because the bank must be prepared both to pay out money to depositors and to accommodate those customers who have a legitimate claim on it when borrowing needs arise, the combination of the dollar figure needed for withdrawals

[20]Reed et al., *op. cit.*, pp. 105-107.

with that which is necessary to make loans represents the total liquidity requirement.

Because the largest commercial banks in the nation are, without exception, members of the Federal Reserve, their contemporary discussions of liquidity necessarily include their actions in response to that agency's regulations. During 1979 escalating demands for bank credit and steadily rising interest rates on all forms of money market instruments resulted in an amendment by the Fed of its Regulation D, which establishes the reserve requirements for member banks. In October 1979 that amendment had a significant effect on the money positions of these major banks. Chairman Paul Volcker of the Federal Reserve Board of Governors, in his statement to Congress regarding the amendment, stated the basic objective: controlling the provision of funds to the banking system to keep monetary growth within established target ranges. The amendment placed a special marginal reserve requirement of 8 percent on increases, above an established October 1979 base, in the larger banks' "managed liabilities" because, in Chairman Volcker's words, "that source of funds has financed much of the recent buildup in bank credit."[21]

Under the language of the amendment, a member bank's managed liabilities include the following major components:

1. All time deposits issued in denominations of $100,000 or more with original maturities of less than 1 year.
2. Certain types of bank obligations, including federal funds borrowings and repurchase agreements, with an original maturity of less than 1 year, issued or obtained in order to fund the banking business.
3. Eurodollar borrowings from foreign banking offices.[22]

Other provisions of the amendment, affecting the operations of foreign bank branches and agencies in the United States, are discussed within the context of multinational banking in Chapter 8.

When the amendment to Regulation D required an increase in reserves for many member banks, it exacerbated an existing basic problem. During the current inflationary period, with interest rates at an all-

[21] *Federal Reserve Bulletin*, November 1979, p. 889.

[22] Supplement to Regulation D, Section 204.5, as amended effective October 6, 1979.

time peak, member banks devoted increased attention to the fundamental question of the real value of Fed membership. Each increase in loan interest rates heightened the realization that substantial bank income could be generated if the reserve funds on deposit at the Fed could be freed up and put to use. Reserves are indeed a component of liquidity, but the burden of maintaining them, and the accompanying opportunity costs, cannot be ignored. Shortly after the announcement of the amendment of Regulation D, a nationwide study showed that 273 member banks thought their withdrawal from the Fed either certain or probable, and 301 others were considering such a move.[23] Every such withdrawal lessens the ability of the Fed to attain its objective of controlling the flow of money and credit.

Safety

No less than liquidity, safety in every phase of a bank's operations is an essential part of its efforts to achieve proper management of funds. Each investment and loan basically represents a commitment of depositors' funds, and those funds must be protected; yet loans and investments carry inherent degrees of risk. If a bank were to overemphasize the concept of safety and choose to take a minimum of risk, it would necessarily confine its operations to those loans and investments that were completely secured by marketable collateral or those that could be sold at a moment's notice. This type of conservatism would reduce income to unacceptable levels, harm the bank's image, and adversely affect many borrowers. By failing to meet the credit needs of its community, the bank might find itself in violation of the basic requirements of the Community Reinvestment Act. Safety, then, is a *sine qua non*, but it must take into account the prudent assumption of certain risks and cannot be considered at the expense of, or to the exclusion of, the other two objectives of managing funds.

Income

Neither can income be overlooked as an objective in this effort. Survival and growth depend on profits. Interest payouts each year, labor costs, and the basic expenses of a bank continue to escalate, and there must be

[23] Phil Battey, "Exodus Threat Grows," *American Banker*, October 22, 1979, p. 1.

a profit margin enabling the institution to offset these and display satisfactory earnings.

However, the fundamental truth that interest on loans is the most important single income factor again comes to the fore. If funds management policies opted to maximize income at the expense of the other two objectives, the bank would necessarily relax its normal credit standards and increase its income by accommodating every category of applicant under every conceivable set of loan conditions. Safety would suffer and liquidity would decrease. Although short-term profits might appear excellent, charge-offs of imprudent loans would, on a long-term basis, create a drain on the entire bank.

BASIC SOURCES

Where do commercial banks obtain the funds with which to conduct their daily operations? There are only three fundamental sources: *capital*, *deposits*, and *borrowings*.

A bank's *capital funds* include the amounts that incorporators originally invested in the institution through their purchases of stock. Retained earnings (often subdivided into undivided profits and surplus) and subsequent issues of common and preferred stock are also part of the capital base. Many banks have also issued interest-bearing notes and debentures in order to build up their captial funds. Instruments of this type have a fixed claim on assets and earnings and have priority over common and preferred stock but are subordinate to depositors' claims.[24] In many cases bank debentures carry the privilege of conversion into stock under predetermined conditions of time and rate.

The amount of a bank's capital is usually thought of as the basis for assessing its financial strength. Capital is the ultimate safeguard against insolvency. Minimum capital requirements for establishing a new bank or opening branches are set forth in federal and state laws; the amount varies according to the size of the community to be served. An examination of any bank by a government agency always includes a determination of its capital adequacy. To bolster stockholders' confidence, most banks stress the amount of their capital funds in their reports and statements and show the additions to those funds during the year.

[24]Crosse and Hempel, *op. cit.*, p. 301.

Under federal and state regulations, the amount of capital is also a determining factor in a bank's credit function. Ten percent of capital and surplus is generally the maximum a bank may lend to any one customer on an unsecured basis.[25]

Deposits constitute the basic raw material of a bank, put to work each day to generate profits and render services. Banks today are funds-gathering organizations that must compete in an increasingly wide and aggressive marketplace for the deposits they wish to attract. Commercial banks remain the prime suppliers of credit to every segment of the economy, and their customers look to them to provide funds in time of need. In order to meet these customer demands, banks must depend largely on deposits; but in today's environment they cannot adopt a passive role and wait for new deposits to appear.

Corporate, institutional, individual, and other types of customers are quick today to take full advantage of the many opportunities available to them. They tend to leave deposits with banks *only* in compensation for services or to gain an attractive rate of interest. The movement of money in our economy from one form of financial intermediary to another has never been more rapid. Disintermediation occurs quickly whenever customers identify more profitable situations. The introduction of MMCs again illustrates this point. When commercial banks were at a competitive disadvantage as a result of the interest rate differential, funds flowed from them to the thrift institutions that offered a better yield. Conversely, when the interest rate differential was eliminated, the flow was reversed. For the same reasons, New York State's mutual savings banks have been experiencing the largest outflow of funds in their history ($779 million in April 1979 alone)[26] because depositors found that money market funds, federal or municipal obligations, or commercial paper were offering higher yields than the banks were legally able to extend.

In seeking new sources of funds, banks may find it difficult to attract additional capital at times when the investment community has strong reservations about their stocks. Efforts to increase deposits may also appear unpalatable if the end result will be a direct increase in interest expense, as is usually the case today. For both these reasons, many banks now turn to *borrowing* as a means of obtaining the funds they need. Bank

[25] Under state laws, state-chartered banks are usually allowed to include undivided profits in calculating their legal lending limit.

[26] *Daily Bond Buyer*, May 15, 1979, p. 3.

borrowings include direct loans made by one institution to another, loans made by the Fed to its members, and federal funds transactions among banks.

Regulation A of the Federal Reserve System pertains to the privilege, held by member banks, of seeking short-term loans directly from the Fed to meet unusual situations or seasonal needs. It states that the use of this privilege over lengthy periods, or on a frequently recurring basis, is not considered appropriate, and in such cases the Fed may simply decline a request.

Whenever the Fed grants credit to a member bank, the loan must be fully secured by either federal government obligations or other eligible instruments. The rate of interest charged by the Fed on these loans is called the "discount rate." Table 4-2 shows the fluctuations in this rate at selected times during the past 23 years.

As noted earlier, the reserve accounts of member banks at the Fed do not earn interest; hence each member attempts to keep its reserve balances at the required minimum level and to put any excess to profitable use. A bank that needs federal funds (also called "fed funds") to meet its own reserve requirement borrows them at the prevailing daily rate.

The then Comptroller of the Currency, James Saxon, issued a ruling

Table 4-2 Discount rate changes of the New York Fed for selected periods

Date	Discount Rate (%)	Date	Discount Rate (%)
8/55	2	5/75	6
8/56	3	5/78	7
9/59	4	6/30/78	7¼
3/68	5	8/18/78	7¾
4/69	6	9/22/78	8
1/71	5	10/13/78	8½
5/73	6	11/1/78	9½
7/73	7	7/20/79	10
4/74	8	8/16/79	10½
2/75	7	9/18/79	11
		10/8/79	12

Source. Federal Reserve Bulletin, November 1979, p. A 8, for figures from 1/71 to 10/8/79. Earlier data from Federal Reserve Board Of Governors, *Annual Monetary Statistics*, 1941-1970.

in 1963 that drastically revised the fed funds market by allowing all national banks to consider transactions of this type as purchases by the borrowing bank and sales by the lending bank. National banks, therefore, were no longer required to show fed funds borrowings as loans on their balance sheets.

With the announcement by Saxon, an entirely new market opened up. Banks that needed funds for their own profit purposes began actively seeking out others that had excess reserves, and the latter found that they could readily sell their surplus reserves to the highest bidder. Table 4-3 shows the results of a survey of twenty-five major commercial banks, including the seven largest members of the New York Clearing House, over a 3-year period. It highlights the importance of fed funds transactions to them during that period and the emphasis on time deposits, rather than the traditional demand deposit base.

Table 4-3 Sources and uses of bank funds, 1971-1973 (in $ billions)

Sources of funds		
Capital and reserves		$5.1
Deposits		
Demand	$13.5	
Time[a]	49.0	62.5
Borrowings		
Federal funds	18.0	
Federal Reserve	0.7	
Others	3.4	22.1
		$89.7
Uses of funds		
Loans		$76.5
Investments		3.9
Other[b]		9.3
		$89.7

Source. M. A. Schapiro & Co., Inc., *Bank Stock Quarterly,* August 1973. Reprinted by permission.

[a]Includes a $31.2 billion increase in large C/Ds.

[b]Fixed assets, reserve requirements, etc.

V

USES OF FUNDS: Wholesale Banking

During 1979, the American Bankers Association embarked on a major new advertising campaign, using television commercials and magazine advertisements to stress the point that the financial needs of every type of customer can be completely satisfied *only* at the nation's 14,000 commercial banks. This advertising is in direct response to the many campaigns conducted by savings and loan associations, brokerage firms, and others to attract funds away from the Full Service banks.

In using "Full Service" to describe the basic nature of their business, the commercial banks are displaying an approach to the market that differs substantially from their traditional limited approach. For most of its history, American banking has been essentially "wholesale" in concept. Networks of bank branches, providing a wide range of services to every category of customer, were largely nonexistent for much of our banking history. The average working person was not thought of as a potential customer, and the entire thrust of banking lay in attracting deposits from large business firms and the lending and investing of those deposits to generate annual profits. To the contemporary observer, who may be surrounded by banks operating hundreds of branches and doing everything possible to market a wide variety of services to every type of customer, it may come as a surprise to learn that widespread "retail" banking is a relatively new development.

By arbitrary definition, the wholesale bank is one that focuses on major corporate, institutional, and government customers. It makes no attempt to be all things to all people. If branching is legally permitted in the wholesale bank's state, it will open only a limited number of branch facilities while its retail competitors' branch systems are being constantly expanded. The wholesale bank's range of services to individuals will not emphasize the installment loan, the Christmas club or similar accounts, and the low-balance checking account, but will concentrate on the trust, investment, and related needs of the more affluent. Fifteen to twenty percent of the wholesale bank's customer base will generate 75 to 80 percent of its deposits.

With the end of World War II, the wholesale banking that had historically characterized the system came under serious questioning. Management began to ask whether that type of banking actually represented the optimum approach to growth and profitability. The consumer came to be perceived as a neglected segment of the total market, and commercial bankers gradually accepted the notion that installment lending need not be left to personal finance companies, that savings accounts for individuals need not remain the exclusive province of thrift institutions, and that individual checking accounts could reasonably be offered to society at large. The relative growth of such competitors as savings and loan associations could no longer be ignored, and a movement that may justifiably be called revolutionary took place in the postwar years.

Where state laws restricted or prohibited branch banking, pressures for legislative change increased as the banks sought permission to function wherever their customers might be. Many banks that had been entirely wholesale in philosophy made the determination that the retail market offered a great deal of profit potential; in several cases they merged with other institutions that had already adopted a retail posture and had succeeded in capturing a share of the consumer market.

This movement was most noticeable in New York City in the late 1950s as one after another of the nation's largest banks announced the completion of negotiations for mergers. The former Chase National Bank, the former Chemical Bank and Trust Company, the former Hanover Bank, and the former Bankers Trust Company merged with the Bank of the Manhattan Company, the Corn Exchange Bank and Trust Company, the Manufacturers Trust Company, and the Public National Bank, respectively. In each case the merger represented a departure for the first-named bank from a wholesale identity and positioned it on the retail side of commercial banking; simultaneously it was able to continue its service to and cultivation of corporate, correspondent bank, institutional, and government accounts. It may be said that the concept of Full Service banking truly began at this time.

WHOLESALE BANKING: BASIC CONSIDERATIONS

From the management standpoint, wholesale banking offers certain inherent advantages. It allows the bank to operate with a relatively small staff, since large numbers of tellers and clerks are not required. It avoids the problems of escalating rent and occupancy costs at a network of branches. By curtailing the transaction volume required by retail banking, it allows the bank to operate with less equipment, requiring less floor space. It creates an image of highly professional specialization and personalized attention to the needs of the clientele.

These putative advantages must be carefully weighed against other considerations. The wholesale bank, by definition, must concentrate on the needs of major corporate, institutional, and government financial officers and recognize the increased degree of sophistication demanded of these individuals. In many cases, the financial officer today finds it possible to bypass the commercial banks—through use of the commercial paper market, for example, in which major firms of unquestioned credit standing use short-term unsecured promissory notes as a means of lending directly to one another[1]—and to reduce the company's dependence on its banks. Any such reduction can be combined with a modern cash management program to minimize the demand deposit balances that the bank would otherwise be given.

An additional risk in wholesale banking lies in the relatively small number of accounts that are maintained for major customers. The loss of any one of these carries significant risk, since it often represents a meaningful portion of the bank's total deposit base. The same reasoning may apply to the credit function at a wholesale bank. The largest firms are inevitably the largest borrowers. Default on any single loan will have a far greater impact on earnings than a charge-off at the retail bank, whose credits are far more numerous and diversified.

[1] As of November, 1979, total outstandings in commercial paper were $109 billion. (*Federal Reserve Bulletin*, January, 1980, p. A25.)

The increasingly multinational aspect of American business compels the wholesale bank to become a global lender, possessing a firm grasp of the current economic conditions in all the areas of the world in which its corporate customers operate. It must be prepared to provide its credit facilities and expertise through such services as international loan syndications and to face the challenges and risks entailed in extensive foreign exchange transactions.

The concept of diversification of risk also extends to concentration of funds from particular industries. A wholesale bank may find that it has become largely dependent on aerospace, automobile, or petroleum firms for its deposits, loans, and income, and a recession or other problem in these segments of the economy significantly affects the entire bank.

A final consideration entering into management's thinking as regards wholesale and retail banking is the degree of volatility of the deposit structure in each case. Savings deposits fluctuate less widely than demand deposits; business accounts display far larger day-to-day balance changes; major corporate, correspondent bank, and government accounts are subject to the highest degree of movement of all. The rate of demand deposit turnover at New York City banks in the early 1970s was seven times higher than the rate in 1945; liability management and liquidity needs are prime concerns in wholesale banking because of this.[2]

VIABILITY

These positive and negative statements may prompt the question whether a wholesale bank can actually succeed at a time when so many competitors are aggressively increasing their retail activity. Two well-publicized contemporary situations may provide an answer.

Morgan Guaranty Trust Company in New York has long been considered the prototype of the wholesale bank. A list of its clientele would include the largest of the "Fortune 500" corporations, as would its portfolio of loans. A spokesman has said that the bank lends to those "Fortune" firms "to whom *we choose to lend.*"[3] His statement reflects the bank's basic philosophy, which calls for providing the highest quality of in-

[2]Howard D. Crosse and George H. Hempel, *Management Policies for Commercial Banks*, 2nd ed., Englewood Cliffs, NJ, Prentice-Hall, 1973, p. 128.

[3]Martin Mayer, *The Bankers*, New York, David McKay Co., 1974, p. 259 (emphasis added).

depth services throughout the world *only* to that segment of the market with which Morgan Guaranty wishes to deal. The bank operates a relatively small number of New York City and worldwide branches, each of which is in an area where its major customers are domiciled and functioning. It makes no effort to saturate the consumer market with installment loans and low-balance checking accounts.

What have been the bottom-line results of this operating philosophy? If compounded annual growth in earnings per share is the criterion, Morgan Guaranty has fared no worse than second among all New York Clearing House member banks during the past ten years, and its first-quarter earnings in 1979 increased 16.5 percent over a very profitable 1978.[4] If, as analysts claim, annual rate of return on each $100 of average annual assets is the performance yardstick, the bank, at $0.74 per $100, ranks first among the ten largest in the United States. It is also far more heavily capitalized than the other nine banks on that list, with total equity 4.8 percent of its average total assets.[5] Lastly, if net income alone is to be used as the measurement of success, Morgan Guaranty ranked third among all commercial banks in 1978 with $248 million.[6] Its success as the epitome of wholesale banking is self-evident.

The second situation is noteworthy in that it evidences a reversal of the general trend away from purely wholesale banking and a significant move in the opposite direction. Bankers Trust Company, a $26 billion institution, transformed itself over the course of some 25 years from a "carriage trade" wholesale bank into an institution serving the needs of every type of customer through a network of 106 branches in the New York City area. However, its Annual Report for 1978 announced management's decision that providing all financial services to all markets was no longer felt to be the optimum course to follow for future profitable growth. Therefore, the Annual Report and subsequent disclosures indicated that Bankers Trust would sell as many as eighty-nine of its branches and would implement a policy of concentrating on and providing services to corporations, governments, financial institutions, and high-income individuals through the remaining branch offices and through the bank's overseas presence in twenty nations.[7]

[4] "Banking Industry's Profitability," *The New York Times*, April 23, 1979, p. D-1.

[5] *Ibid.*

[6] Mark F. Polanis and Barrett F. Binder, "The Top 50 Profit Performing Banks," *Bank Administration*, October 1979, pp. 37-40.

[7] Robert A. Bennett, "Bankers Trust: Corporate Focus," *The New York Times*, April 16, 1979, p. D-1.

Bankers Trust's decision resulted from a planning process similar to that described in Chapter 3. The bank conducted a self-examination to identify its strengths and then selected the segments of the market to which those strengths were best suited.[8]

None of the foregoing material should be construed as an effort to polarize the wholesale/retail concept and thus to indicate that banks must make an either/or decision in this regard. Indeed, there has been a widespread trend away from the purely wholesale system, and commercial banks today generally want to be known as Full Service institutions that do not focus on major corporations to the exclusion of other types of customers. The typical bank today attempts to combine the best elements of both wholesale and retail banking. The institution identifies those types of customers with whom it believes it can most effectively deal, then selects the services that can best be rendered to them on a profitable basis.

An example of this can be seen in those banks that have restructured their organizations to create Corporate Banking Departments. An officer in one of these units works parallel to his counterparts at the wholesale bank, but his department is only one part of a larger organization whose other components address the needs of "middle market" businesses, lower-income individuals, and other customers in the area served by the bank. An institution that is described as retail in its orientation should not be thought of as one that neglects corporate business, but rather should be considered as diversified in comparison with a wholesale bank.

USES OF FUNDS: CREDIT

Archaeologists have uncovered evidence of a loan made by representatives of a temple in ancient Babylon to a local farmer who promised to repay the loan, with interest, after the harvest. In *The Merchant of Venice* Shakespeare created Shylock as the archetypal moneylender who accomodated local merchants. In England goldsmiths often acted as private bankers, extending credit to their customers. Truly the borrowing of money is as old as history itself.

The American Revolution was largely financed by borrowing, and since that time our country has to an increasing extent been one that

[8]Bankers Trust New York Corporation, *Annual Report*, New York, 1978.

operates largely on credit. The commercial banks, which in the course of history came to replace the temples, goldsmiths, and other lenders, are the major suppliers of that credit. Measured against a gross national product of over $2 trillion is the fact that gross loans at the nation's commercial banks were over $843 billion in September 1979.[9] Whether a bank is characterized as wholesale or retail, large or small, and regardless of the size and nature of the geographic area in which it functions, it always recognizes a responsibility to satisfy the legitimate credit needs of its customers and community. In doing so, it not only provides a needed service but also generates the profits necessary to its survival and growth.

Which customers of banks create these demands for a continually increasing supply of credit? This can be conveniently answered by considering three segments of our society: federal, state, and local governments; businesses; and individuals.

Governments must resort to various forms of borrowing in order to meet their increased expenditures. The federal government, of course, is the bellwether in this respect, since in only 3 of the years that have elapsed since 1951 have revenues exceeded spending. The total gross public debt is now in excess of $826 billion, and Congress has found it necessary to raise the statutory debt limit five times since 1976 to make additional borrowing possible. Federal budget deficits have in some instances exceeded $68 billion in a single year.

As a group, commercial banks are by far the largest holders of all types of federal government debt issues. FDIC statistics for all insured commercial banks disclose that at year-end 1978 these institutions held $89.6 billion of direct, fully guaranteed U.S. government obligations (Treasury bills, notes, and bonds) and an additional $42.3 billion in obligations of other federal agencies.[10] The total, $131.9 billion, represented 10.3 percent of the assets of these banks.

State and local entities of government face the same chronic problem. They cannot raise taxes or develop new sources of income to keep pace with expenditures. In 1978 municipal governments issued over $48 billion in new obligations.[11] Again, the commercial banks were the prime suppliers of credit, maintaining their role as the major holders of munic-

[9] *Federal Reserve Bulletin*, November 1979, p. A15.
[10] Gerald C. Fischer, "The Commercial Bank Balance Sheet, 1960-1985," *Journal of Commercial Bank Lending*, Philadelphia, Robert Morris Associates, October 1979, pp. 52-53.
[11] *Federal Reserve Bulletin*, November 1979, p. A36.

ipals. Their investments in these debt issues at year-end 1978 were $123.5 billion, or 9.6 percent of total assets.[12]

Businesses of every type and size continually resort to bank borrowings to meet their seasonal, working capital, capital expansion, or other needs. Despite the efforts of many corporate financial officers to use commercial paper or other methods to borrow, the commercial banks remain in a preeminent position as the source of credit. Of the total gross loans of $843.5 billion reported by all commercial banks in September 1979, $285.8 billion had been loaned to businesses.[13]

Individuals make up the third category of bank borrowers and use various forms of credit far more readily and extensively today than ever before. Total installment debt of consumers has been increasing by over $3.3 billion per month (average) through the first 7 months of 1979 and has reached an all-time peak figure of $303.9 billion, of which $148.7 billion was owed to commercial banks.[14] In addition to this, $814.9 billion is outstanding in mortgage debt on 1-to-4-family homes, of which commercial banks hold $229.6 billion.[15]

The financing of these three major categories of borrowers has largely been provided by commercial banks despite the extent and ready accessibility of their competition. Thrift institutions, retailers, credit card issuers, commercial and personal finance companies, credit unions, brokerage firms, and insurance companies are all active in the lending field in various ways; yet commercial banks continue to dominate, chiefly because they alone have the capability to offer every size and type of loan to every segment of the borrowing marketplace under every conceivable set of conditions. As our inflation-fueled economy has grown steadily in the years since World War II, so has the overall credit function at commercial banks, and the emphasis that had formerly been placed on investments has declined proportionately. A bank's first obligation in the use of funds is to its creditworthy customers; all other uses have lower priority. Although loans and investments may both be considered by a bank as extensions of credit, they always rank in that order. Loans always have priority when banks allocate funds; investments rank

[12]Fischer, *op. cit.*, pp. 52-53.
[13]*Federal Reserve Bulletin*, November 1979, p. A15.
[14]*Ibid.*, pp. A42-43.
[15]*Ibid.*, p. A41.

below them and must possess marketability so that the bank may sell them at any time to fund its loan portfolio.

In 1950 total loans at all insured commercial banks were 31 percent of their total assets. By 1960 that percentage had risen to 47, and when nationwide demands for credit reached previously unheard-of levels in 1974 total loans were 60 percent of total assets.[16] The September 1979 figures for all commercial banks indicate that total loans of $843.5 billion represent 63 percent of total assets.[17]

Although the credit function is an integral part of the daily operations of all Full Service banks, and although these institutions regularly make various types and sizes of loans to the three basic categories of borrowers, it is invariably the corporate customers who are the largest depositors and the major users of credit. For this reason, the credit function is considered here as most relevant to wholesale banking. Consumer credit of all types warrants separate treatment, and is dealt with in Chapter 6.

BASIC CONSIDERATIONS

The most simplistic definition of a commercial bank would state that it accepts deposits and puts them to work to generate profits. Deposits, then, are the basic raw material, and in this regard the bank is tantamount to a manufacturer who converts the goods furnished by suppliers into a finished product to be sold at a profit. There is an essential difference, however, that results from the relationship of a bank to its customers.

Those who supply raw material to a manufacturer never expect to recover it; those who supply money to a bank insist on that right of recovery. Every deposit, even if it is considered to create an asset because it can be put to profitable use, remains a liability, since at some time, in some fashion, it must be returned to the customer.

Therefore, the considerations of liquidity, safety, and income directly affect the credit function at commercial banks. At all times, the bank must simultaneously attempt to meet the legitimate credit needs of its community and its customers—especially those corporations that have

[16]Edward W. Reed, Richard V. Cotter, Edward K. Gill, and Richard K. Smith, *Commercial Banking*, Englewood Cliffs, NJ, Prentice-Hall, 1976, p. 141.
[17]*Federal Reserve Bulletin*, November 1979, pp. A20–21.

long-standing relationships and supply much of the bank's deposit base—and to be in a position to honor all orders from depositors for withdrawal or payment of funds. The bank's options are severely limited if it cannot meet these twin goals on any given day. It may be forced to liquidate part of its investments, perhaps at a loss; or it may resort to borrowings in order to obtain the working funds it needs. As a last resort, it may call in some outstanding loans, to the extreme detriment of customer relationships.

During periods of high economic activity, the rate of deposit turnover and the demand for credit often escalate at the same time, creating intense pressures on the banking system. When this occurs while the deposit base is shifting from a demand to a time orientation, the problem increases in magnitude. Banks today must not only seek to attract and retain deposits in order to function; they must also derive maximum yield from their loans and investments to offset the rising costs of purchased funds. Yet the quest for yield, especially in lending, can easily lead to deterioration in the loan portfolio if the bank relaxes its criteria and accepts borrowers who would otherwise be rejected.

The interrelationship of loans and deposits is such that the ratio between them is frequently used as a yardstick, determining the extent to which banks are called on to use available funds. Although much has been written regarding the increase in demand for credit in 1978 and 1979, the year 1974 is of even greater interest, since it provides a classic example of responses by banks to the problems of managing funds. Table 5-1 traces the historical pattern of ratios of loans to deposits to the point at which they reached unprecedented levels.

During 1974 every category of borrower displayed an increasing demand for bank credit, and total lending at each of the nation's nine largest commercial banks increased by at least 21 percent over the prior

Table 5-1 Loan to deposit ratios

Year	New York City Banks	All Commercial Banks
1950	37.9	33.7
1960	54.7	51.2
1970	70.2	65.2
1974	78.5	72.3

Source. Edward W. Reed, Richard V. Cotter, Edward K. Gill, and Richard K. Smith, *Commercial Banking*, Englewood Cliffs, NJ, Prentice-Hall, 1976, p.120.

year; at year-end four of those banks showed loan-to-deposit ratios of 80 percent or more.[18] One bank Chairman admitted, in referring to 1974, "We were guilty of excesses. We got caught up in giving analysts a thrill a minute."[19] It became evident that the banks, in their desire to meet as many credit requests as possible and to improve profits by accommodating every borrower, neglected many of the fundamentals of credit. Paul Nadler's comments were particularly critical:

> Every bank was on a drunken kick—buy your money, diversify, liability management, high multiples.[20]

The result was the charging off of some $2 billion in loan losses for the year 1974, including some $382 million that was charged off by the five largest banks alone.[21] In addition to that immediate consequence, long-term problems were created, many of which remain unresolved. Some condominium loans made in Puerto Rico, some credits extended to the governments of the emerging nations, and some of the financing extended to real estate investment trusts remained in workout status five years after the actual lending took place.

In retrospect it is difficult to realize why the banks embarked on this course of credit expansion at a time when so many adverse signals could be seen. An OPEC embargo on oil shipments to the United States had existed from October 1973 to March 1974. Unemployment had risen rapidly, housing starts had decreased from over 2 million units annually in 1973 to 1.3 million in 1974, and the nation was experiencing double-digit inflation. Both financial and nonfinancial businesses found their liquidity positions weakened. The federal government let it be known that there had been a very meaningful increase in the official "watch list" that identified problem banks. That list was said to contain not only new bank names but also historic ones, including some of the industry giants. Within a short time the banking community was severely shaken by the news of the closing of Bankhaus Herstatt in West Germany and the failures of the United States National Bank, a billion-dollar institution in San Diego, and the Franklin National Bank in New

[18]"The Great Banking Retreat," *Business Week*, April 21, 1975, p. 78.
[19]*Ibid.*
[20]In "The Great Banking Retreat," *Business Week*, April 21, 1975, p. 78.
[21]Stanley Strachan, "Banks Dig in for Shaky Loans," *The New York Times*, February 2, 1975, p. BUS-1.

York. These events combined to create a very real lessening of confidence in the entire banking system.[22]

The year 1974 has been emphasized here negatively, because it was a year in which basic credit considerations seem to have been bypassed in favor of expanded profits. However, 1974 was not without its beneficial effects. It brought about a reappraisal of basic policies and a return to more prudent operations. Its events have become part of a learning process, the result of which has been renewed emphasis on all aspects of *quality*—quality of credit analysis, quality of administration in the loan portfolio, and quality of funds management.

THE LENDING PROCESS

If the millennium ever arrives and banking attains its utopia, a simple, foolproof set of guidelines will have been developed to remove all elements of risk from the credit function. Unfortunately, no such ready formula has ever been developed. Except in those few cases in which a loan is fully secured by cash collateral or some other form of immediately marketable, guaranteed security, risk will always be present. An unforeseen event may convert what appeared to be an acceptable credit situation into a charge-off. Business recessions occur, manufacturers suddenly find that their products no longer sell, and even units of government overextend themselves.

The objective of the lending process, properly implemented, is not to attempt to achieve zero losses, but rather to accept the fact that losses will sometimes occur and to take every prudent step to reduce that possibility. There is no magic formula guaranteeing a good loan, but there are certain procedures that can keep risk to a minimum. Conversely, the bank that neglects these procedures will inevitably suffer losses.

The lending process logically begins with a clear understanding of the loan purpose. Why is the customer requesting this accommodation? Is the purpose consistent with established bank policy? Does the purpose make the loan subject to government regulation, as in the case of loans secured by stock market collateral and made to buy or pay for other listed securities? Is there some indication that this same purpose will be

[22]Fischer, *op. cit.*, p. 59.

used again in a future loan request, as in the case of a borrower who requires repeated infusions of bank credit to meet working capital requirements? In addition to establishing the purpose of the loan, the bank should make every effort to identify the specific projected source of repayment. The clearer this identification, the more likely it is that the loan will not evolve into a workout situation.

In some cases, the attempt to identify a source of repayment is neglected on the grounds that collateral is being tendered. This is unsound. Good collateral lends strength to a credit request but of itself should not provide the rationale for approval. Loans should be collectible from the borrower's inflow of income and profits. A bank should not rely on the collateral alone. Deterioration of collateral may occur, as in the case of listed securities that are subject to stock market fluctuations. Forced sales of collateral often yield less than the outstanding loan amount and frequently serve as evidence that the loan was weak at the outset.[23]

Because unsecured loans make up by far the largest portion of a bank's portfolio, constant and thorough attention must be paid to the area of credit analysis. Gathering as much financial data as possible regarding a corporate borrower is an integral part of the process of identifying sources of repayment. The bank's own credit files may serve as the starting point. They provide a history of the customer's relationship with the bank and include correspondence, interviews with members of the company's management team, and data on balances, overdrafts, and prior loans. This step in the decision-making process may be supplemented by investigations conducted with the borrower's other banks and trade suppliers. Audited financial reports should be obtained wherever possible.

The work of a loan officer in credit analysis includes evaluation of the borrower's character and managerial ability, review of the firm's history of sales and earnings, and detailed consideration of the balance sheet, income statement, liquidity, return on assets, and cash flow.[24] The loan officer should ask whether the company appears able to generate cash by selling bonds or equity. Such critical ratios as debt to total assets,

[23]Crosse and Hempel, *op. cit.*, p. 170.

[24]Charles F. Mansfield, Jr., "The Function of Credit Analysis in a U.S. Commercial Bank," *Journal Of Commercial Bank Lending*, Philadelphia, PA, Robert Morris Associates, September 1979, p. 24.

debt to net worth, current assets to current liabilities, and past-due receivables to total receivables should be calculated.[25]

Implementing bank policy is also an integral part of the credit process. Based on liquidity, safety, and income considerations, and in keeping with regulatory constraints and money market conditions, the bank's directors and senior managers establish guidelines for loan officers to follow. Merger or acquisition loans, for example, may be deemed unacceptable. Certain loans that contribute to community well-being may be made as part of the social responsibility program. As a policy matter, the level of compensating balances expected from corporate borrowers may be adjusted. If audits disclose that many demand loans[26] are being allowed to remain on the books indefinitely, the bank may implement a policy requiring each such borrower to remain out of its debt for an annual 30-day period. Factors in the money market may dictate acceptance or rejection of requests for long-term credits. These, and all other policies, are not to be considered as straitjackets applied to loan officers. There should be some degree of flexibility, but any exceptions or changes should be consistent with the overall planning process.

Interest Rates

A further area of bank policy entails setting the interest rates that may be appropriate at various times. In retail banking, the ability of management to set these rates is often restricted by state laws, as in the case of installment loans, home mortgage loans, and credit card outstandings. In wholesale banking, interest rates may be more readily adjusted as money market conditions change. Essentially, money is a supply-and-demand commodity; its availability sets the price that must be paid for it. The term "profit margin" has particular relevance here in view of the fact that commercial banks now depend heavily on their purchased funds to carry out their credit function. The spread between the cost of such funds and the yield obtained through lending or investing them is critical to profitability. The Federal Reserve discount rate is generally

[25] Reed et al., *op. cit.*, p. 180.

[26] Demand loans are loans made without a fixed maturity date, callable by the bank or repayable by the borrower at any time. They give the bank the advantage of revising interest rates whenever necessary; time loans are usually made at fixed interest rates.

considered a base for other interest rates. On a hypothetical ladder of rate structures, the prime rate, charged by commercial banks to their largest and most creditworthy customers, would stand immediately above the discount rate. During 1979 the spread between the discount rate at the New York Fed and the prime rate ranged from a low of 1½ percent to a high of 3¾ percent.[27]

In recent years there has been some criticism of the fact that a major corporate customer pays interest at the prime rate whereas borrowers of lesser stature are penalized by being forced to pay higher rates. This criticism is predicated on the assumption that large corporations are less adversely affected by high rates, since they can readily recover their borrowing costs by increasing their product prices. Smaller businesses presumably would find this more difficult.

The rebuttal to this argument states that it is imprudent to allow customers of lesser credit standing to borrow at a preferential interest rate vis-à-vis a "Fortune 500" corporation. In response, some banks have instituted a two-tier prime rate system in which major corporate borrowers have one rate and customers of smaller size have another, lower rate.[28]

Interest rates that mirror market conditions and are applied impartially are generally accepted by the borrowing public as a "sign of the times" and do not necessarily inhibit borrowing, especially in periods of tight money. There is evidence to support the belief that customers do not necessarily complain about high interest rates per se; rather, they take exception to the idea that other borrowers receive preferential treatment and that rate discrimination therefore is in effect.[29]

The introduction by some major banks of "floating prime rates" tied directly to money market instruments, and revised regularly, has been a positive step in convincing the borrowing public that banks themselves do not directly establish the cost of money. Citibank, N.A., in New York and First National Bank in Chicago have been the pioneer banks in implementing this system, and their periodic announcements of prime rate changes, in accordance with a publicized formula, are watched closely as important indicators of money market trends.

[27] *Daily Bond Buyer*, November 2, 1979.
[28] Mayer, *op. cit.*, pp. 422-423.
[29] Crosse and Hempel, *op. cit.*, p. 198.

Loan Classification

To meet the reporting requirements of government agencies and for their own management information and internal control purposes, commercial banks have used various methods of categorizing all their wholesale loans. Some common examples include classification by maturity, industry, security, and type of borrower.

In classifying loans according to maturity, the basic breakdown is between time and demand loans. The former may then be subdivided into short-term (i.e., less than 1 year) and long-term. Ninety-day loans are the most common single type, reflecting the fact that liquidity needs compel banks to emphasize short-term lending.

By monitoring loans made to various industries, management can avoid the risk entailed in an undue concentration. When global or domestic events affect a particular industry, it is essential that the bank know its credit position as regards companies in that field so that appropriate policy decisions can be made.

Loans may be categorized as unsecured or secured, and the latter group may be subdivided to show the type of collateral. If necessary, a further breakdown can show specific concentrations of collateral, such as the dollar amount of outstanding loans secured by shares in one particular stock.

The usual classification of borrowers includes the broad grouping of commercial and industrial loans, made to businesses of all types; interbank loans and participations, which are loans to a single borrower shared by two or more banks; real estate loans, which are subdivided into construction loans and long-term mortgage loans; and installment loans to consumers.

Interbank loans today consist chiefly of Fed funds transactions. As noted previously, national banks need not report these as direct borrowings; however, bank management may wish to list them as such to show the extent to which fed funds are a source of supply. By obtaining these funds from other banks, members have been able to reduce significantly their borrowings from the Federal Reserve itself.

Participations may result from the fact that a loan request exceeds one bank's legal limit, from that bank's practical desire to diversify its credits, or from the borrower's decision to divide a loan among several banks at which accounts are maintained. The situation of the W. T.

Grant Company offers a classic example. When the company filed its bankruptcy documents, it disclosed a single loan of $700 million, shared by 136 banks. Three major New York City banks had extended $97.5 million each.[30]

Real estate loans steadily increased in amount and importance during the 1970s as a thriving economy seemed to require more office buildings, apartment houses, shopping centers, and single-family homes. Construction loans are short-term and provide developers with the funds needed to complete the project. They are made only when the developer is able to demonstrate that he has already obtained permanent financing, which is the mortgage type of real estate credit and is made with the property itself as collateral. Much of the overexpansion of the real estate industry in the 1950s was fueled by Real Estate Investment Trusts (REITs) that, in turn, obtained financing from banks. When many of the condominiums, office buildings, and other REIT projects proved incapable of generating sufficient income to permit repayment of the debts, the REITs were forced to default on their own obligations to the banks and in some cases had no choice but to declare bankruptcy. During the single year of 1974, commercial banks loaned $5 billion to REITs, much of which was not recovered.[31]

BANK INVESTMENTS

The management of funds at commercial banks operates on a strict priority basis. Liquidity needs must be satisfied first so that provision is made for possible withdrawals of deposits and expansion of the loan portfolio. Only then can management turn its attention to those investment possibilities that are legally permitted and can be looked on purely as a source of income.

In some cases bank investments are made to provide additional secondary reserves. U.S. Treasury bills, for example, carry no credit risk, are short-term, and are immediately marketable. They provide income while contributing to bank liquidity.

Other bank investments must be made in order to meet regulatory constraints and special requirements of customers. Some state laws, for

[30] Stanley Strachan, *op. cit.*

[31] "The Federal Reserve: Doctor to Sick Companies," *Forbes*, February 1, 1975, p. 24.

example, call for commercial banks to hold federal or state obligations amounting to 110 percent of all state deposits.[32] In other cases the required amount is not as large, but the principle prevails: public funds deposited with the banks must be backed up by guaranteed federal or state obligations so that no loss of those funds can ever take place.

A third category of bank investments includes the obligations issued by local communities. In buying these the bank assumes a higher degree of credit and market risk, but it also gains the significant benefit of exemption from federal tax on the investment income and simultaneously enhances its image as a good citizen in the community. By buying the municipality's debt issues, the bank is helping the community to finance local projects and meet local needs, thus giving recognition to the fact that its own growth is closely tied to that of the geographic area it serves. Local governments naturally tend to place their deposits with banks that have invested in their debt issues.

Legal Considerations

The Banking Acts that were passed by Congress in 1933 to reorganize and strengthen the industry imposed several constraints on the banks' investment functions. Banks were prohibited from any investment in common stocks for their own portfolios. Their holdings of the obligations of any issuer except the federal government were limited to 10 percent of capital and surplus. The Glass-Steagall Act allowed banks to underwrite general obligation bonds of a municipality when the full taxing power of the issuer was pledged to guarantee repayment. These are commonly known as "full faith and credit" issues, and banks today are leading underwriters in the field. The same legislation, however, prohibited any underwriting of revenue bonds, which are secured by the income from bridges, tunnels, highways, and other fee-earning municipal facilities. This is an important contemporary topic, since the commercial banks are actively seeking repeal of the Glass-Steagall Act. In 1978, 60 percent of all municipal financing was in the form of revenue bonds. This percentage can be expected to increase, due to voter pressures, as municipalities place greater emphasis on user charges for services and less emphasis on direct taxation. The commercial banks have taken the position that they can render a direct, substantial benefit to municipal

[32]Reed et al., *op, cit.*, p. 325.

financing programs if they are legally allowed to compete with securities firms in underwriting revenue bonds.

Investment Planning

A commercial bank's investment portfolio consists almost entirely of Treasury bills, notes, bonds, and municipal issues. The mix within the portfolio may be adjusted on a daily basis, according to liquidity needs and money market conditions. Because a bank must make every effort to accommodate its customers in times of high demand for credit, it may reduce its investment portfolio, even if such sales are made at a loss, and uses the proceeds for loan purposes.

During World War II commercial banks were not faced with heavy loan demand from corporate customers; they were therefore able to build up substantial portfolios of U.S. government obligations. From 1941 to 1945 these holdings increased from $22 billion to $91 billion.[33] In the immediate postwar years, the banks continued to focus most of their investment attention on these same obligations, the price of which was supported by the government itself. The 1951 Accord brought about a change in strategy. Banks began to look more favorably on municipal bonds as investments, and the advantages they offered from the standpoint of federal income tax became more important as the banks' mix shifted from demand to time deposits. When time deposits, creating direct interest expense, increased, investment income was necessary to offset the costs of doing business. From 1959 to 1964 commercial banks' total deposits grew by some $80 billion, three-quarters of which was in time and savings deposits; during the same period, their investments increased by $23 billion, but the percentage of U.S. governments in their portfolios had declined from 75 to 62.[34] By 1974 the 331 major commercial banks that are used for Federal Reserve reporting purposes had restructured their investment portfolios to such an extent that they held $49 billion in municipal issues and only $24 billion in direct obligations of the federal government.[35] This 2-to-1 ratio was still valid in

[33] Reed et al., *op. cit.*, p. 343.

[34] Leland S. Prussia, Jr., "Bank Investment Portfolio Management," in Herbert V. Prochnow and Herbert V. Prochnow, Jr. (Eds.), *The Changing World of Banking*, New York, Harper & Row, 1974, p. 155.

[35] M. A. Schapiro & Co., Inc. *Bank Stock Quarterly*, May 1974.

September 1979.[36] The major commercial banks in New York City alone hold over $9 billion in various municipal issues.[37]

Contemporary topics of discussion among bankers relate this shift in portfolio emphasis to the basic questions of risk and social responsibility. Does a bank's obligation to provide maximum safeguards for the funds entrusted to it by depositors supersede its obligation to support a community that is in obvious financial difficulty? Should the same credit criteria be applied to corporations and municipalities? Does a bank's civic responsibility require that it lend to its own community and that it do so at preferential rates? Is a bank justified in demanding repayment of debt by a municipality when its own future profitability and growth presumably are tied to that same municipality? These questions pose challenges to the ingenuity, tact, and good judgment of bank management. Conflicts will inevitably arise. Civic activists will point out that no municipality has actually defaulted on any debt issue since the Depression; yet depositors will want assurance that their funds are being invested with all due consideration for safety and prudence. The fiscal crises experienced by New York City in 1975, Cleveland in 1978, and Chicago in 1979 may sound a warning signal, prompting banks to take new approaches to the subject of investing in municipals. These may dictate that municipalities disclose their operations in more detail, adopt more uniform accounting practices, accept the thesis that they are expected to identify specific sources of repayment whenever they borrow in any manner, and possibly give the investing banks more voice in municipal budgeting.

[36] *Federal Reserve Bulletin*, November 1979, p. A22.
[37] *Ibid.*

VI

USES OF FUNDS: Retail Banking

Throughout the first 160 years of American banking history, the commercial banks systematically rejected the average individual wage-earner as a customer. Conversely, in the 35 years that have gone by since the end of World War II, a continuing and massive effort has been made to reverse that posture and do everything possible to attract consumers. New services are continually being developed to meet the needs of the retail banking customer. The working person who traditionally found the doors of major commercial banks closed now finds that he or she is a prime target for cultivation and that every type of electronic and automatic facility is being provided to make banking more convenient and attractive. The commercial banks, as a group, have developed a totally new relationship with the individual customer during the postwar years.

Although wholesale banking remains the keystone of the system and corporate, government, and correspondent bank and other institutional relationships will never be neglected, there are many examples of the ongoing trend toward more and more retail cultivation. New marketing campaigns have been mounted to convince John Doe and Mary Jones that commercial banks are indeed people-oriented. Intense lobbying has brought about amendment of many of the state laws that restrict branch banking, and wherever this has occurred new branches have proliferated. From 1950 to 1970 the number of commercial banks in America remained essentially unchanged, but the number of branches grew from 19,000 to 34,000; during the decade of the 1960s alone, the number of branches more than doubled.[1] In New York State alone, where state laws on branching were liberalized on two occasions, the statistics graphically demonstrate this trend[2]:

Year	Number of Banks	Number of Branches
1950	635	1390
1970	283	3067
1977	239	3414

Where legally possible, banks have tended to follow the population. The growth of the suburbs and the movement of industry out of the central cities have opened up new territories for banks.

RETAIL MARKETING AND COMPETITION

The dynamics of change in banking philosophy can also be seen in the multitude of ways in which the perceived needs of the individual are being addressed. An individual today can take advantage of a host of services that were never before made available. He or she may be encouraged to apply for an installment loan by telephone, obtain currency from an automated teller facility where this is legally permitted, use a bank card for an infinite variety of goods and services, pay bills by telephone, obtain a personal line of credit to accompany a free checking account, receive a mortgage or home improvement loan, or buy a small-denomination, nonnegotiable savings certificate. As he or she becomes more affluent, additional services, such as personal investment management and counseling, may be made available.

[1] R. Gene Conatser, "Retail Banking" in Herbert V. Prochnow and Herbert V. Prochnow, Jr. (Eds.), *The Changing World of Banking*, New York, Harper & Row, 1974, p. 189.
[2] New York State Bankers Association, personal communication.

Largely as a result of their efforts to publicize retail services, commercial banks in America spent ten times as much on all forms of advertising in 1971 as in 1950.[3] As many as twelve different types of checking and savings accounts have been identified at a single bank. These and all the other facilities that are now readily available to individuals are extensively publicized through every form of mass communication: radio and television commercials, magazine advertising, urban and suburban newspapers, and throwaway handouts announcing the opening of new branches or the expansion of services. Banks that formerly used only low-key, "tombstone" advertising, and that to a limited extent, now employ full-page newspaper advertisements and billboards. The traditional bank philosophy, holding that the world knew where the bank was located and would seek it out whenever necessary, has disappeared.

As Walter Wriston has noted, it is ironic that many financially oriented organizations that were always among the commercial banks' major customers have now become their aggressive competitors in the retail marketplace.[4] The small-denomination notes that Sears Roebuck intends to sell to the public, the combination cash management and investment account that Merrill Lynch is offering, and the mortgage-backed securities that Salomon Brothers intends to sell are but a few examples. Beneficial Financial Company owns both a commercial bank in Delaware and a savings and loan association in Texas; it also markets its own credit card.

Savings and loan associations, often unhampered by the plethora of federal and state laws restricting commercial bank operations, now place their on-line terminals in supermarkets so that their clients can obtain currency, make deposits and withdrawals, and debit purchases to their account balances—all without the need for visits to the association's premises. Credit unions now include some 25 percent of all American households among their membership. They are offering 30-year home mortgage loans, credit cards, certificates of deposit, and "share drafts" for bill payments.[5]

In today's society, more individuals have higher incomes, are better educated, more sophisticated, and better candidates for commercial bank services than at any time in the past. A major current topic of

[3]"Now Banks Are Turning to the Hard Sell," *Business Week*, June 24, 1972, p. 78.
[4]In "Consumer Banking," *Business Week*, April 23, 1979.
[5]*Ibid.*

discussion is the attempt to identify the ways in which this growing market can best be served by the banks in the face of extensive and aggressive nonbank competition. As part of that discussion, some thought must be given to a basic change in the life-style and philosophy of the individual customer.

Incurring debt may have carried a stigma in the minds of past generations of Americans, who made their purchases only when they had accumulated the necessary cash. No such reservations on borrowing exist in today's social structure. "Buy now, pay later" has become one of the more widely used phrases in the national vocabulary, and the average consumer displays no reluctance whatever to incur additional debt, even if his or her financial resources have already been strained. Personal bankruptcies and installment loan delinquencies have increased in recent years, yet every type of lender continues to encourage borrowings and consumers quickly take advantage of the availability of all types of credit. In a single month—September 1979—consumer installment credit increased by $4.4 billion, attaining an all-time high of $303.9 billion exclusive of mortgage debt.[6]

In an era of double-digit inflation, it appears likely that individual debt will continue to increase as consumers borrow today and expect to repay with tomorrow's "cheaper" dollars. Nadler[7] attributes this expansion of consumer debt to fears of further price increases,—that is, loans should be obtained now to buy the appliances, automobiles, and other goods that will cost 10 to 15 percent more next year.

The extent to which borrowed funds contribute to the growth in gross national product may be judged from the receivables reported by six major nonbank lenders at year-end 1978, in billions of dollars[8]:

General Motors Acceptance Corporation	$25.6
Ford Motor Credit Corporation	14.1
General Electric Credit Corporation	6.0
Sears Roebuck and Company	5.1
CIT Corporation	4.1
Household Finance Company	3.1
	$58.0

[6]*Federal Reserve Bulletin*, November 1979, p. A42.
[7]In "Banking in Transition," *The Bankers Magazine*, September-October 1978, p. 26.
[8]*American Banker*, June 11, 1979, p. 5.

The $58 billion owed to these six organizations gives rise to speculation about the portion of this debt that commercial banks could have assumed had they been able to overcome the inherent advantages possessed by nonbank lenders. In contrast, New York City commercial banks as a group had total outstanding (commercial, industrial, and consumer) loans of $45 billion at year-end 1978.[9]

Again, whether because they chose to neglect home mortgage loan applicants per se for many years, or because there were periods when interest rates made such loans unattractive, commercial banks lag behind their competitors in this retail area. Their mortgage outstandings on 1-to-4-family homes at June 30, 1979 were $136 billion; savings and loan associations had outstandings of $378 billion.[10] Especially when recent increases in real estate values are considered, this may be viewed as another lost opportunity.

However, any criticism of the banks for shortfalls in performance versus that of other lenders should be tempered by a realization of the disadvantages under which they operate. Finance companies and other lenders who extend $58 billion to consumers can freely cross state lines, but interstate banking is prohibited by federal law. Savings and loan associations do not face the same restrictions imposed on commercial banks by federal and state authorities. Nonbank lenders have few concerns over Federal Reserve requirements or controls.

Nevertheless there are many retail service areas in which commercial banks have displayed remarkable growth in recent years. The world's most profitable financial institution, Bank of America, was a pioneer in the retail banking field, since California's laws allowed it to open branches wherever its customers were. Its retail operations generated 50.6 percent of total net income ($514 million) in 1978.[11] Although other commercial banks cannot match that performance, there is much evidence of the increased extent to which they have expanded their retail operations. The installment loan is a prime example.

INSTALLMENT LENDING

The unsecured monthly-payment installment loan, granted to a typical wage-earner, literally did not exist in commercial banks until the 1920s,

[9] *Federal Reserve Bulletin*, May 1979, p. A22.
[10] *Ibid.*, November 1979, p. A41.
[11] "Consumer Banking," *Business Week*, April 23, 1979, pp. 82–83.

and at year-end 1945 accounted for only 7.5 percent of total bank loans; by 1971 that percentage had tripled.[12]

Entry into the installment loan field can be an expensive effort for a bank. Credit investigation units and specialized accounting and collection departments must be established to supplement the work of the officers or other platform personnel who interview applicants; coupon books or other repayment media must be obtained and advertising must be initiated. The investment, however, is justified by the typical results. In the abstract the installment loan borrower may open his or her personal checking and savings account, rent a safe-deposit box, or use other services. More concretely the lending bank looks to a substantial contribution to income from its installment loan operations. Such loans are usually discounted—that is, the full interest for the entire life of the loan is collected by the bank at the time the loan is made. The overall loss experience of banks in the installment loan field has been very favorable.

The consumerism prevailing in today's society is reflected in many of the federal and state regulations affecting installment lending. Annual percentage rates (APR) must be clearly stated, so that if the loan is discounted the borrower is made aware of what it is actually costing. Documents must be written in simple, clearly understandable language. Reasons for declining a loan must be disclosed. Collection practices must conform to certain standards. Federal Reserve Regulation B has been amended to require that banks give full weight to an applicant's pension, alimony, or income from part-time work.[13] The Equal Credit Opportunity Act of 1976 prohibits discrimination on the basis of sex, race, marital status, color, religion, national origin, and age.

Many banks have developed credit scoring plans to assist them in the decision-making process. These systems assign numerical values to various attributes, such as home ownership, length of employment, income, and current fixed debt payments.

The consumer today is likely to be besieged by various forms of bank publicity encouraging him or her to take advantage of installment loan availability. This promotional material may stress the fact that a loan at one bank does not preclude borrowing from another or that the repay-

[12]Howard D. Crosse and George H. Hempel, *Management Policies for Commercial Banks*, 2nd ed., Englewood Cliffs, NJ, Prentice-Hall, 1973, p. 176.
[13]"Amendment to Regulation B," Federal Reserve Bank of New York, Circular 8564, April 1979.

ment terms for automobile loans have been extended. This approach is not without its critics.

Social and philosophical questions arise as to the overall effect of the commercial banks' expansion of installment lending. Consumer installment credit now includes $148.7 billion owed to these banks,[14] and much of this has been used to purchase home appliances, cars, and other goods, thereby contributing to total GNP and improving the borrowers' standard of living. At the same time, the banks' promotional efforts may have had the effect of lulling consumers into a false sense of security by creating the impression that debt can be expanded indefinitely or that repayment need not be a matter of real concern. The actions of the banks in 1974 have been cited in this regard.

During the "credit crunch" of that year, every type of bank borrowing increased dramatically. Growth in installment lending was part of the syndrome. Banks made no real effort to curtail this, nor did the Fed act to curb their expansion.[15] Delinquencies on installment loans rose sharply, and some observers were severely critical of the fact that banks were "urging—almost begging—families to sign up for open lines of credit." The point was made then, and is relevant today, that banks that display no restraint in lending cannot expect consumers to display restraint in borrowing.

PERSONAL BANK ACCOUNTS

Until the immediate postwar years, checking accounts at commercial banks were reserved for business firms, institutions, government agencies, and the more affluent individuals who could maintain appropriate balances. The introduction of the so-called special checking account, requiring no minimum balance but carrying monthly and per-check service charges, was another manifestation of the banks' new approach to the retail market. Although the name "special" may have fallen into disuse, the type of account continues and is now offered by commercial banks throughout the country. The largest banks have hundreds of thousands of these and frequently offer them as part of combination plans that tie them to other bank services.

[14] *Federal Reserve Bulletin*, November 1979, p. A42.

[15] By its failure to act, the Fed came under attack for fueling inflation. See Martin Mayer, *The Bankers*, New York, David McKay Co., 1974, p. 344.

"Cross-marketing" has become the norm in retail banking. Each monthly statement sent to a depositor may be accompanied by promotional material for other services. An installment loan borrower automatically becomes a candidate for an account and is often able to gain a preferential interest rate by authorizing the bank to charge the account for monthly payments. When a personal account is opened, the bank may develop a profile sheet to give its marketing staff an indication of other services for which the new customer is a likely prospect. Existing bank customers always generate much of the new business, and by stressing the Full Service concept to depositors an institution can tie itself to a depositor in many ways.

Two surveys, sponsored by The Foundation for Full Service Banks, were conducted by Louis Harris and Associates in 1970 and 1972. In the 2-year interval between them, consumer use of checking accounts at commercial banks increased from 68 to 76 percent among respondents. Savings account usage increased from 67 to 73 percent, use of safe-deposit boxes from 21 to 26 percent, and use of drive-in facilities from 39 to 45 percent.[16] A similar study today would no doubt show increased consumer usage of many other retail banking facilities, such as NOW accounts, telephone bill paying, sales of traveler's checks and foreign currency packets, personal money orders, and Series E bonds. The introduction of MMCs in 1978, mentioned earlier, offers another example of liability management, this time through the retail market; these certificates accounted for $104.4 billion of total personal investments in early 1979, of which commercial banks held $31.9 billion.[17]

BRANCH BANKING

When commercial banks turned their attention to the consumer market in the postwar years, their new emphasis on retail services necessarily carried with it the notion that branch banking would have to expand for the convenience of customers. As noted earlier, many banks that had formerly been wholesale in orientation expanded into branch banking by merger, and wherever it was legally possible under state laws they

[16]Louis Harris, *The Second Study: The American Public's and Community Opinion Leaders' Views of Banks and Bankers in 1972*, Philadelphia, The Foundation for Full Service Banks, 1972, p. 8.
[17]"Regulation Q," Federal Reserve Bank of New York, Circular 8534, March 9, 1979.

steadily increased their branch networks. Recently, however, this basic philosophy has come under intense questioning.

The overall concept of profit planning includes the creation of individual profit centers, each of which can be assessed according to its contribution to the overall success of the bank. In the case of branches, bottom-line figures can be developed for each. If the branch's deposits exceed its loans, it is a supplier of funds to the rest of the institution's "pool" and is given credit for the excess at prevailing rates. If its loans exceed its deposits, it is a net user of funds and must obtain them from the bank pool and be charged accordingly. If the bank is restructured internally so that corporate accounts are housed in a single central department rather than in the branches, the figures must be revised.

As rental, equipment, and labor costs increase, many banks have begun to ask whether full-scale "brick and mortar" branches are actually needed to meet the needs of retail customers and whether the number of existing branches should be reduced. The range of retail services need not be curtailed, but the manner of delivering them may change as less costly techniques are developed. There is increasing emphasis today on automated facilities, operating throughout the year 24 hours a day. These represent an expensive initial investment, but on a long-range basis eliminate many of the costs created by actual branches. Storefront loan-producing facilities or check-cashing installations may replace the large, expensive branches that were formerly established to serve the public.

As interest payments and expenses escalate, it is incumbent on bank management to reassess its thinking about the advisability of maintaining some of the branches that no longer make adequate contributions to overall earnings. Perhaps two or three branches were optimistically opened in the same geographic area and can now be combined. Perhaps the potential business in a community was overestimated, and subsequent data prove that it is no longer profitable to compete there. Where significant demographic changes have occurred in an area, there may no longer be a sufficient number of customers to make the branch worthwhile. If internal reorganization has transferred corporate and institutional accounts away from branches, the end result may be a decision to close some of them. For those that remain, management may consider the feasibility of confining their services to those segments of the retail market that can be expected to be profitable. Lastly, the opening of savings bank and savings and loan branches, or nonbank facilities, in a community may have gained so many customers that commercial bank competition is no longer feasible. As a Federal Reserve Governor asked rhetorically, "Once a man can cash a check at a local supermarket, what does he need a branch for?"[18]

However, a word of caution must be interjected on the subject of branch closings. Community activists may use the concept of social responsibility as their rationale for demanding that a branch be kept open, even if it is unprofitable. Bank spokespersons must be both forthright and tactful in explaining why such branches actually constitute luxuries that can no longer be afforded.

In some cases, as in the well-publicized decision of Bankers Trust Company in New York, management makes a determination that organizational resources can best be focused on the corporate, institutional, and other wholesale markets. If the network of branches, once viewed as potentially highly profitable, is to be cut back, other banks that intend to concentrate on retail business may purchase the facilities.

BANK CARDS

In the face of the tremendous acceptance attained by bank cards in recent years, it is perhaps difficult to appreciate that they constitute a recent development in commercial banking. Yet, with the exception of some minor efforts made by banks in the 1950s to emulate the success that gasoline companies, Diners Club, airlines, and hotel chains had achieved in the credit card field, there was no concerted effort made until the mid-1960s.

The rationale for the banks' entry into the field at that time becomes apparent if viewed in the context of the economic climate that prevailed. Large sums of money were leaving commercial banks in favor of other, more attractive investment media. Those deposits that remained were shifting toward a time, interest-bearing basis, creating new expenses. Banks felt compelled to develop new forms of high-yield business and new retail inducements. The improvements in computer technology made it possible for them to process huge volumes of paper at relatively low cost.

The credit card, as it was then known, appeared to offer a most attractive profit potential. Increased deposit activity would result from the sales slips turned over to banks by merchants. Cardholders would

[18]Mayer, *op. cit.*, p. 180.

pay interest at a high rate on their outstandings. A discount on each deposited sales slip would generate additional direct income. When cards were used to obtain cash advances, an immediate interest charge could be levied. And although commercial banks, by federal law, could not branch across state lines, they could issue cards on a nationwide basis, thus attracting new customers.

Today two major bank cards dominate the field. As of September 30, 1979, VISA reported 61 million domestic cardholders, while Master Card reported 59 million. Total outstandings at that date were $11.8 billion and $11.2 billion respectively. Master Charge cards are issued by 11,485 banks; VISA cards by 11,253.[19]

According to all indications, bank cards possess still further opportunities for growth. There are over 3000 banks that are not yet issuing cards, but that may jóin either system or both. Issuers of travel and entertainment cards may withdraw from the market and thus provide bank cards with new opportunities. Present cardholders may increase their usage as they find new areas of acceptance. The bank card is the key to many EFTS applications, including automated teller facilities.

Two major nationwide marketing efforts were initiated in 1979. Citibank, N.A., in New York sent out 27 million VISA card solicitation letters; Continental Illinois (Chicago) offered consumers up to $3.5 billion in credit through a campaign to attract new customers for both cards.[20] The fact that both disregarded state boundaries is seen by some observers as a step toward eventual interstate banking. A cardholder who has been granted a personal line of credit and can obtain cash through use of a card issued by a bank many miles away may no longer feel that a local account is needed. The same card can be used for local purchases. This potential creates fears in the minds of many independent bankers in smaller communities that the consumer system will be monopolized by large, money-market-center institutions.

Historical Development

For banks that are entering the card field, there is a critical dilemma that must be resolved. In the early 1960s, those institutions confronting this problem chose a course of action that proved disastrous.

The dilemma lies in the fact that merchants can be induced to join a

[19]Jeffrey Kutler, "Bank Card Usage," *American Banker*, January 7, 1980, p. 2.
[20]"Consumer Banking," *Business Week*, April 23, 1979, pp. 82-83.

card plan only if they are convinced that the cards are already in the hands of an army of cardholders who are anxious to begin using them. At the same time, individuals realize that the new cards have no value unless merchants are ready to accept them. A management decision must be made about the best manner of addressing this question.

In one well-documented instance, a number of major banks in the same large city simultaneously reached a decision to begin offering cards and chose to do so by flooding the population with their new form of "plastic money." They purchased mailing lists from many sources and conducted unsolicited mailings of cards to each name on each list. No attempt was made to verify the accuracy of addresses or to weed out duplications. No credit investigations were conducted, and no limitation was placed on the dollar usage of any card. The mass mailings of millions of the new cards took place at the peak of the city's Christmas mail rush.

This ill-conceived and poorly executed program resulted in widespread thefts of cards from the mail and their repeated uses by the thieves, receipt of many cards by a single individual, and uncontrolled usage of the cards to buy quantities of merchandise, sometimes with the collaboration of unscrupulous merchants who were guaranteed payment by the card-issuing banks. Direct losses of over $7 million in 6 months were sustained by the banks involved in this effort.[21]

The early history of the card program contains many other examples of problems experienced by major banks. A New York commercial bank admitted losses of $8.4 million in 2 years from card operations, while a California bank conceded that it had lost $7 million in 3 years.[22] These reports served to convince other banks not to enter the card field at all.[23]

These historical developments, however, have not caused widespread abandonment of the card as an integral part of retail banking. Rather, there has been a systematic effort by the banks to correct the weaknesses and resolve the initial problems. This effort has been supplemented by considerable legislative action, affecting many phases of bank card operations.

As a policy matter, most banks today establish criteria for the issuance

[21] A detailed history of this case may be found in Mayer, *op. cit.*, pp. 347-348, and in Harold S. Taylor, "The Chicago Bank Credit Card Fiasco," *The Bankers Magazine*, Winter 1968, pp. 49-52.

[22] Irwin Ross, "The Credit Card's Painful Coming of Age," *Fortune*, October 1971, pp. 108-111.

[23] R. Gene Conatser, "Retail Banking," in Prochnow and Prochnow, *op. cit.*, p. 199.

of any new card and restrict its use to a specified dollar limit. Strict security measures have been imposed on the operations units where cards are mailed out and records of outstandings and payments maintained. In many cases banks will not mail new or renewed cards, but will require that the cardholder visit the bank and sign for the card. Merchants can obtain prompt answers through computer installations when they inquire about a cardholder's status. Some banks have included a photograph as part of the card itself, and both VISA and Master Charge have established national networks for prompt credit verification.

Legislators have also acted to protect consumers against loss of their cards and subsequent unauthorized use. A cardholder who promptly reports loss or theft of a card cannot be held responsible for its use. The maximum interest that can be charged on outstandings is restricted by state usury laws. Furthermore, all unsolicited mailing of actual cards is prohibited.

As in the case of installment lending, expansion of the bank card field has created fears among some observers that consumers are actually being encouraged to go even more deeply into debt and to embark on programs of foolish and excessive purchases.

There is no doubt that the bank card, now used for 6 percent of all consumer-initiated payments in the United States (including those made in cash),[24] has given the public a new, widely accepted tool to be used for obtaining needed or wanted goods and services. It may have given rise to the fears mentioned in the preceding paragraph by accelerating and facilitating impulse buying.[25] At the same time, it has eroded a portion of what would have otherwise been installment lending, since the consumer can use it spontaneously for purchases instead of planning those purchases in advance and obtaining a loan to cover them.

Yet, on balance, whatever real or perceived problems may exist in the overall scenario, it remains true that the bank card is becoming a permanent fixture in retail operations. There is increasing evidence that the cardholder, assuming appropriate criteria have been met, can be trusted to confine his or her usage to reasonable levels and makes every effort to repay the obligations created by that usage. This parallels the

[24] R. Michael Rice, "The Growing Consumer Debt Burden," *Bankers Monthly Magazine*, April 15, 1979, p. 35.

[25] Peter J. Gray, "The Case for Credit Cards," *The Bankers Magazine*, July-August 1978, p. 27.

banks' experience with the installment loan itself. Furthermore, by learning from the mistakes that were made in the early days of card marketing and operations, the banks have been able to reduce their loss ratios and, in many cases, to make the entire card function a source of net profits.

By providing the consumer with attractive, useful alternatives to the former payment and borrowing system, by creating a source of ready emergency cash for the cardholder, and by opening the door to a new world of banking by acting as the key to automated facilities, bank cards have come to represent a most important element in retail banking. A major bank in Philadelphia, reporting that it has increased its market share of households in a highly competitive urban area from 15 to 18 percent in 5 years, emphasizes the role of the bank card in its success. The bank has implemented automated teller facilities at many of its locations, each of which requires use of a card, and offers customers a single consolidated statement, showing every transaction for the period, including all bank card usage and current outstandings. By coupling these retail services with bank-by-phone capability, and by converting some of its traditional branches into "mini-branches," this institution has met the challenges of contemporary retail banking and made its total program profitable.[26]

SELF-SERVICE BANKING

The aforementioned success story exemplifies the most readily identifiable trend in retail banking today: the effort by banks to allow retail customers to conduct their business at the time and location of their choice, often without any interface with bank personnel. There are three major self-service areas: point-of-sale devices, customer-operated devices, and banking at home. The entry of banks into these three areas is, in turn, driven by three critical factors.

First, the cost structure of retail banking now demands new ways of conducting business. Costs for both personnel and property have increased at an annual rate of some 7 percent, making greater efficiency mandatory if the retail banking program is to generate profits.

Second, the introduction of new technology has made new services

[26] Richard S. D'Agostino and Harold Y. Jones, "Retail Banking: The Girard Approach," *Bank Administration*, June 1979, p. 28.

not only feasible but economically attractive. Prices for the equipment needed for self-service banking have decreased substantially.

Finally, the retail market has changed, and banks must respond to that change. One recent study comprises 48 percent of all U.S. households; it estimates that the individuals who were demographically surveyed will display far more sophistication toward, and acceptance of, electronic devices.[27] The manner in which banking services can be offered to them in future years is part of the new world of banking—a world largely dependent on all that the acronym EFTS (Electronic Funds Transfer Systems) implies.

[27] Marc J. Frankel, "Self-Service: An Emerging Trend in Retail Banking," *Chase Directions*, New York, The Chase Manhattan Bank, N.A., Fall 1979, p. 2.

VII

ELECTRONIC FUNDS TRANSFER SYSTEMS

Early in the twentieth century, American telephone companies increased their marketing efforts, stressing all the advantages of telephone service for every type of user. Their campaigns were so successful that an entirely new technology had to be developed to handle the volume of telephone calls. The manual format, in which an operator personally placed every call, gave way to the dial telephone, and the latter, in turn, has undergone many further enhancements needed to support customer usage.

Similarly the nation's brokerage firms, as they became aware of the increased level of American family income in the postwar years, introduced a succession of advertising campaigns to attract new investors. The stockholder base of many corporations consequently grew, as did the volume of purchases and sales each day. The brokerage firms found themselves swamped with a "back office" volume beyond their capacity as a result of the promotional campaigns they themselves had conducted. "Fails" (transactions in which purchased securities were not properly delivered) became so common that many firms had to be liquidated.

In both cases an industry sold its services to the public, only to find that it could not cope with the transaction volume generated by its own efforts. Both situations may have influenced the thinking of bankers during the 1960s.

Banking has always been a paper-intensive field, with the check as its most widely used document. Normal annual growth in check volume in the years prior to World War II was handled with no great difficulty, and in the immediate postwar period this increase did not give rise to any real concern. The assumption was that the system would automatically be able to meet customer demands.

The growth of the postwar economy gradually brought about a change in thinking. Check usage increased at an unprecedented rate. Businesses expanded and required more checks to pay more suppliers. Checks replaced cash as the method of paying employees. Retail marketing efforts brought a new type of customer into the banks; the checking account was no longer a vehicle used only by the more affluent. The average consumer—more sophisticated, better educated, and with a higher level of income than his predecessors—came to recognize the advantages of checks as payment instruments.

As check usage steadily increased, fears were expressed that the banking system would prove unable to cope with the volume. The introduction of the magnetic ink character recognition system, with its accompanying automated technology for check processing, allayed these fears only for a short time. Predictions of imminent calamities in the system began to be heard. Bankers wondered if their industry might suffer the same fate as the brokerage firms and find itself submerged in a sea of paper, with consequent delays, errors, and increases in processing costs. A study, conducted in 1970 for the American Bankers Association, projected annual increases of 7 percent in check volume for the remainder of that decade.[1] One individual, recognized as a data processing authority, claimed to have originated the phrase "checkless society" to indicate the direction in which he felt banks would have to move—that is, they would have to find a substitute for checks as payment media.[2]

To some extent statistical evidence supported these fears and predictions. Check volume in 1948 had been 5 billion; by 1976 it had increased to 26 billion, and the most recent figures refer to an annual volume of 30 billion checks.[3] Although several prominent bankers ex-

[1] Wray O. Candilis (Ed.), *The Future of Commercial Banking*, New York, Praeger, 1975, p.117.

[2] Dale Reistad, speech delivered at the Bill Payment Workshop, New York, December 1977.

[3] Alfred L. Hunt, *Corporate Cash Management and Electronic Funds Transfers*, New York, AMACOM, 1978, p. 139.

pressed confidence that the industry could cope with these increases, pressures for change continued and new approaches to the payment system were sought.[4]

Costs were an important consideration. A study conducted in Atlanta in 1972 showed that checks cashed or deposited at the drawee bank (and therefore completely processed in-house) created per-item costs of $0.103; checks that had to be routed to other banks cost $0.137 each.[5] More recently it has been estimated that the entire life cycle of a check costs the issuer $0.55, including postage and handling charges.[6]

In retrospect it now appears that in many cases commercial bankers, equipment designers, consultants, and systems experts were caught up in a syndrome of overreaction in which each group vied with the others in projecting a totally new world of banking. A new society was envisioned on the assumption that all types of bank customers would enthusiastically adopt the latest technology. Checks would be eliminated, and visits to banks would be made unnecessary by the installation of computer terminals in customers' homes and offices, supermarkets, and other key locations.

These prophesies have been only partially fulfilled. There are, indeed, areas where EFTS services have been introduced with considerable success, offering benefits to both the bank and user. However, as a generalization, it appears that the early forecasts of universal adoption of EFTS were totally unrealistic. Instead of using the earlier phrase, "checkless society," today's bankers speak of a "less-check" system in which checks will be used, but in greatly diminished quantities. Evolution, rather than revolution, has taken place.

As a generic term, EFTS (or EFT) has become one of the most widely used acronyms in banking. It originally stemmed from the initial letters of electronic funds transfer systems. Some bankers have modified this by substituting the word "services" for "system." In either case the reference is to a broad spectrum of automated technology that uses bookkeeping entries for the movement of funds among financial institutions.

The emphasis on EFTS has been so great that entire libraries are now devoted to its reference material. It is undoubtedly one of the most significant topics in contemporary banking. Questions continually arise,

[4]David Van L. Taylor, "Banking Technology More Paradox Than Panacea," *American Banker*, May 22, 1979, p. 7.

[5]Candilis, *op. cit.*, pp. 118-119.

[6]Hunt, *op. cit.*, p. 151.

and opinions are expressed, regarding the extent to which it is likely to gain acceptance, the effects of regulatory constraints and pending or potential legal action, and the degree to which nonbank financial institutions will participate.

For purposes of this text, the focus is on four fundamental EFTS applications:

1. Systems that produce *credits* to accounts.
2. Systems that generate *debits*.
3. Systems that entail use of *point-of-sale terminals*.
4. Systems that entail use of *automated teller machines* (ATMs) or *customer-bank communication terminals* (CBCTs).

In each case the known reactions of actual and potential users are discussed. To provide a fully balanced presentation of this critical topic, both positive and negative viewpoints are analyzed.

EFT CREDIT SYSTEMS

In April 1968 members of the local bank clearing house associations in Los Angeles and San Francisco determined that the future progress of EFTS required their establishing automated facilities, analogous to their check-handling counterparts but processing magnetic tape instead of paper checks. The Subcommittee on Paperless Entries (SCOPE) began operation of the first automated clearing houses (ACHs) in the two cities in October 1972.[7] Similar installations were established in Atlanta (1973) and Boston and Minneapolis (1974), and by 1978 twenty-seven additional ACHs were functioning in key cities. They accept magnetic tape in a standard format created by banks or corporate debtors or creditors. The tape contains all identifying data on each payment: dollar amounts, names of the parties involved, and bank and customer account numbers. The tapes submitted to each ACH are then used to generate new tapes for savings and commercial banks, savings and loan associations, and credit unions that participate in the system.[8]

The ACH effort reflected the banks' concern over steadily increasing

[7]"California's Step Toward Checkless Banking," *Business Week*, September 9, 1972, p. 56.
[8]Carl M. Gambs, "Automated Clearing Houses," *Economic Review*, Federal Reserve Bank of Kansas City, May 1978, p. 4.

check volume, and by year-end 1977 over 9 million monthly payments were being processed at ACH installations.[9] Although this figure indicates that growth in EFT activity has been steady, it must also be disappointing to those who had predicted much greater acceptance of the system. SCOPE, for example, projected a volume for 1977 of 8 million monthly EFT transactions from the private sector alone, whereas an analysis of actual activity showed that 85 percent consisted of payments from the federal government.[10]

It made eminently good sense for Washington to assume a leading role in EFT credits. In the 20-year period from 1958 to 1978, civil service retirement payments tripled, railroad retirement payments doubled, veterans' payments increased 15 percent, and monthly check usage for Social Security rose from 7 million to 32 million.[11]

Aside from the sheer volume of statistics, the Treasury Department recognized the costs involved. An analysis conducted in the early 1970s indicated that in-house costs for each check issued were $0.18. The Department was also processing over 1 million claims per year from individuals who denied having received federal checks. On behalf of the Treasury's Fiscal Service Unit, Plumly summarized the official viewpoint:

> We had no palatable alternative to the development of a better means of coping with continually increasing workloads. At the same time, we needed a more positive payment delivery system. And lastly, it has become more and more difficult to attain higher productivity and reduce consumption of resources under the check disbursement system.[12]

In late 1973 the federal government announced the start of its first EFT system test, under which Air Force personnel were invited to begin receiving direct deposits of wages and salaries at the banks or other financial institutions of their choice.[13] The success of this test led the Air Force to move ahead with total conversion of its payroll.

[9] *Ibid.*

[10] Gambs, *op. cit.*, p. 5.

[11] Les Plumly, "Electronic Funds Transfer of Federal Recurring Payments," paper presented at the First Annual Cash Managers Conference, New York, April 12, 1978.

[12] *Ibid*, p. 2.

[13] Since the inception of EFTS, user participation has been optional. Most recently, Title IX of the Financial Institutions Regulatory Act of 1978 bans any compulsory use of EFTS, and the National Commission on Electronic Fund Transfers has suggested that no individual should be forced to accept an EFT service or be required to open an account in order to do so.

In February 1976 the second stage of federal adoption of EFTS began with the direct depositing of 51,000 payments to Social Security beneficiaries. By 1979 this monthly volume had grown to over 9 million, of which 62 percent went to accounts at commercial banks.[14]

The TreasuryDepartment has every intention of continuing its efforts to expand the present system and has set a goal of 18 million monthly payments by mid-1981. Direct deposits of federal employees' pay and income tax refunds are among the areas from which this growth is expected.[15]

To some observers the success of the government effort provides evidence that the new world of banking is actually here and that the use of checks for such purposes as payroll will disappear. Acceptance by so many Social Security recipients gives rise to the assumption that other segments of the population will make the same choice.

However, in actual practice this has not proved to be the case. The Social Security beneficiary has certain characteristics that the wage-earner lacks. Most such recipients have checking accounts or savings accounts, so that direct depositing is easy to arrange. They are vitally concerned that each monthly payment be received on time, since their standard of living is dependent on prompt availability of funds. They may have had problems with lost or stolen checks, experienced mail delays in receiving payments, or had difficulty cashing a Social Security check.

The office or factory worker does not fit this same profile and has displayed no overwhelming desire for direct depositing of his or her net pay. There have been some noteworthy exceptions, but these have chiefly involved management personnel. A recent list of corporations that have implemented direct deposit of payroll includes the names of Allied Chemical, Aluminum Company of America, Dow Chemical, IBM, and American Motors, yet each of these has applied it only to managerial salaries and at most is "exploring its application" to other categories of employees.[16] Considerable consumer skepticism still prevails among many wage-earners, who seem to feel that it is simply another way in which corporations obtain benefits for themselves while taking advantage of employees.[17]

[14]Daniel Cowles, "U.S. Makes 9.7 Million Payments," *American Banker*, April 2, 1979, p. 2.
[15]Plumly, *op. cit.*, p. 2.
[16]"Improvements in Automated Clearing House Services," Federal Reserve Bank of New York, Circular 8572, May 17, 1979.
[17]Hunt, *op. cit.*, pp. 150-151.

Advantages of Direct Deposit

For the typical employee direct deposit of payroll offers as its chief advantages timeliness, convenience, and security. Individuals who agree to accept it are given a guarantee by their bank that the net pay will be credited on the stipulated payday, even if the necessary input tapes have not been received. Direct deposit eliminates the possibility of stolen, lost, or fraudulently negotiated payroll checks and the need for payees to spend time cashing them. A further benefit exists for those employees who have used the services of private check cashing firms; direct deposit avoids the per-check charges levied by these firms.

The potential benefits to the payer may not be as significant. The time and expense involved in actual payroll check preparation can be eliminated, but the statements showing earnings, deductions, and year-to-date figures must still be prepared. Some corporations have stated that as long as these reports must be generated in any event, there is little additional cost in also issuing a check. They also point to the fact that direct deposit requires timely creation of input tapes for the ACH; this is considered tantamount to preparing an actual check.[18]

In addition to payroll activity, many firms have considered direct deposit for dividend and pension checks. In these instances postage costs are a major factor, and the circumstances that make the recipient of Social Security a likely candidate apply. General Motors, Allied Chemical, American Motors, and National Cash Register Corporation were recently reported to be planning implementation of direct deposit for these purposes.[19]

Opposition to Direct Deposit

For a variety of reasons, acceptance of direct deposit has never been as widespread as anticipated. Despite bank guarantees, employees seem to fear that their net pay will not be available on the specified date and believe that rectifying any error will be far more difficult under EFTS.[20] Past experiences may have conditioned them in this respect. Many Americans have been the victims of computer errors that caused incorrect bills, repeated and erroneous nonpayment notices, deliveries of

[18]"Checkless Banking," *Business Week*, September 9, 1972, p. 56.
[19]Federal Reserve of New York, Circular 8572, May 17, 1979.
[20]Candilis, *op. cit.*, p. 131.

unordered goods, or unsatisfactory credit reports. The impersonality of computer systems and the problems and delays encountered in correcting mistakes negatively affect attempts to market EFT credits.

A study conducted in 1972 by COPE, the Atlanta Committee on Paperless Entries, identified twenty-seven separate areas of consumer resistance to EFTS; loss of personal control was most frequently mentioned.[21] The study highlighted the fact that many wage-earners want their net pay in cash or a check, which give them privacy and control. A system that makes information regarding net pay (including overtime, bonuses, and incentive payments) available to other household members, through credit advices or bank statements, is anathema to them. Employees do not appear to consider check cashing at banks a sufficient hardship to warrant converting to direct deposit. This is especially true when state laws compel employers to allow paid time for this purpose. Other resistance to direct deposit comes from the 20 percent of American households operating on a cash basis, without checking accounts. These families generally purchase money orders for bill paying, and see no valid reason for changing their financial pattern.[22]

From the payer's viewpoint, an objection to direct deposit has been voiced by corporate financial officers who actively manage daily "float." Payroll, dividend, and pension checks are mere entries in a disbursement register until they are actually presented to drawee banks and debited to accounts. The corporate treasurer who keeps demand deposit balances to a minimum has very little interest in a system that entails immediate debiting—a process that takes place as soon as tape input is processed by an ACH.[23]

EFT DEBIT SYSTEMS

In view of the reservations expressed by many consumers regarding direct deposit, including loss of control and fear of computer errors, it is perhaps surprising to find that private debit transfers have become a rapidly growing form of EFTS. In December 1977 739,000 such trans-

[21] *Bank Systems and Equipment*, November 1972, p. 54.

[22] Gambs, *op. cit.*, p. 10.

[23] Paul S. Nadler, "The Human Side of Electronic Banking," *Bankers Monthly Magazine*, May 15, 1978, p. 12.

fers, usually involving movement of fixed, recurring sums from individuals to businesses, were processed. Most of these represented payments to insurance companies, but standardized payments for home mortgage or personal loans, and regular contributions to dues-collecting organizations also achieved some degree of acceptance.[24] Consumers evidently are willing to adopt the debit system when predetermined amounts must be paid to meet important obligations on specified dates.

The EFT application to insurance payments was pioneered by the Equitable Life Assurance Society, in collaboration with the Chase Manhattan Bank in New York. This program has received widespread publicity. The insurer periodically prepares magnetic tapes containing all necessary data on those policyholders who have authorized account debiting. These tapes are delivered to Chase, which initially uses them to debit the accounts of its own depositors. Chase also prepares a single credit to Equitable for the dollar total of all payments on the tapes. The bank then forwards the remaining data through ACH facilities to over 1500 financial institutions throughout the country. Each of these then debits its own policyholder accounts. The success of this system has led other insurers to implement similar plans.[25]

The "Bill-Check" system offers another example of innovative technology in processing consumers' debits. It enables a bill payer to examine each invoice rendered by suppliers of goods and services and to return part of that invoice to his or her bank as authorization for payment. Funds are then directly transferred from the consumer's account to the supplier's. When this proposal was first outlined in the Atlanta questionnaire prepared by COPE, it generated the highest degree of acceptance, among 1375 respondents, of all the services listed.[26]

Advantages of EFT Debits

Under certain circumstances, EFT debits are now known to possess advantages that make them more easily marketable than some other forms of funds transfers. They eliminate the direct costs of checks, the time and effort required to prepare and issue checks, postage expense, and the fear that a critical payment will not be made when due. The transaction

[24]Gambs, *op. cit.*, p. 8.

[25]George C. White, Jr., "Electronic GIRO Payments," *American Banker*, October 14, 1976, p. 5.

[26]Candilis, *op. cit.*, p. 129.

cost to the consumer is generally far less than the per-check charge levied by the drawee bank. Such fixed, recurring obligations as insurance, home mortgage, and installment loan payments readily lend themselves to the EFT debit system because the consumer has advance knowledge of the amount owed and the timing of each payment. His or her essential element of control is preserved. It is these benefits that banks must stress if growth in the system is to continue.[27]

For the insurance company, department store, bank, public utility, or other recipient of a large volume of payments, EFT debits offer substantial benefits. If a payee has been receiving checks directly, the costs of opening mail, examining checks, and preparing timely deposits must be incurred. If the payee uses lock box service through a bank or banks, compensating balances must be maintained to pay for the service or direct fees must be paid. EFT debits address this entire problem. They reduce the payee's direct and indirect expenses and provide quicker availability of funds with greater assurance of actual payment, since the risk of returned checks is minimized. Direct tape input for computer posting of receivables is a by-product of the EFT debit system. Efforts by businesses to cooperate with banks in marketing the debit concept can be anticipated as the benefits become more widely appreciated.[28]

Opposition to EFT Debits

Why has the EFT debit system grown much more rapidly than the credit system? This question becomes even more interesting if one considers the opposition that was manifested in the early stages of the program. The Louis Harris study of 1972 showed that some two-thirds of the respondents were opposed to any form of automatic bill payment from their bank accounts,[29] and senior officers of both Citibank and Security Pacific National Bank (Los Angeles) publicly stated that their banks' customers would probably have very strong reservations about the system.[30] Repeated surveys of the consumer marketplace identify fears of a loss of control over financial affairs resulting from EFTS.[31] The

[27]Robert E. Knight, "Cautionary Notes on EFTS," *American Banker*, September 25, 1974, p. 4.

[28]Gambs, *op. cit.*, p. 12.

[29]*The Second Study: The American Public's and Community Opinion Leaders' Views of Banks and Bankers in 1972*, Philadelphia, The Foundation for Full Service Banks, 1972, p. 123.

[30]"Obstacles to National EFTS," *American Banker, September 25, 1974, p. 4.*

[31]Gambs, *op. cit.*, p. 11.

slow development of the SCOPE project has been attributed to the banks' failure to take this basic attitude into consideration.[32]

A study conducted by one of the largest accounting firms reinforced much of this opposition. It identified consumer reluctance to "do business with a machine," fears that unauthorized debits might be posted, and an awareness of the float benefits inherent in the check payment system. Sophisticated individuals today know how to use float to their advantage and, like their corporate financial counterparts, are reluctant to lose this benefit.[33]

There is an element of irony in the EFT debit program, as Nadler[34] has pointed out. In marketing checking accounts commercial banks always mentioned the advantage to the customer in having paid checks as proof positive of payments. Recently the same banks are attempting to convince consumers that no such "receipt" is necessary, and the EFT debit advices will serve equally well. One aspect of consumer resistance involves uncertainty over this point.

The growth in acceptance of EFT debits, despite all the evidence of consumer apathy or hostility, can be attributed to two fundamental causes. The first involves the *types* of debits that have made that growth possible. The statistics cited earlier give evidence of carefully restricted usage; almost exclusively the program succeeds when applied to payments that pertain to important obligations, do not vary in amount, and recur at regular intervals. Conversely, consumers tend not to accept the system in its broader aspects. If they feel that scrutinizing a bill carefully and timing its payment are important, they resist the program of EFTS debits. Recipients of bills rendered by credit card issuers, utilities, and department stores usually want to examine each invoice, especially if their past experience includes computer-related errors.

The second reason for the acceptance of the debit program can be traced to the many protective *constraints* that have been sequentially imposed on it. Regulation E (12 CFR 205) of the Federal Reserve System was amended on two occasions during 1979[35] to provide the consumer with additional safeguards. It specifies that "reasonable advance

[32]Mayer, *op. cit.*, p. 174.

[33]Peter D. Louderback, "Who's Afraid of EFT?," *World*, Peat, Marwick, Mitchell, Autumn 1977, p. 47.

[34]"The Human Side of Electronic Banking," p. 14.

[35]Federal Reserve Bank of New York, Circular 8619, August 8, 1979 and "Electronic Fund Transfers," Federal Reserve Bank of New York, Circular 8669, October 29, 1979.

notice" must be given if the amount of a preauthorized payment is to vary beyond a predetermined range. The consumer has the right to stop payment, orally or in writing, on any preauthorized transfer up to 3 days before the payment is to be made. Section 4-404 of the Uniform Commercial Code has also been revised so as to treat stop payments on preauthorized transfers on the same basis as those on checks and other instruments.[36]

The effect of these and related federal and state statutes has been to allay some of the fears and doubts originally expressed by consumers. Placing legislative restrictions on the debit system may also help to convince users that the nation's financial institutions are not assuming complete control over their payment procedures.

An additional area of EFT-related services is the GIRO method of payment. It is analogous to the Bill-Check system and has been successfully implemented in several European countries, either through the local postal service or through banks. In essence, it is a system under which a bill payer instructs a bank to make direct payments of funds to the account of a payee. It enables the consumer to gain the benefits of automatic transfer while retaining full control.

In the GIRO system businesses use a standardized bill format, containing a special data field. Optical Character Recognition (OCR) typeface is used so that the bill can be read by automated equipment. The bank and account to which funds are to be transferred, the type of payment and dollar amount, and the payer's identification are encoded in this field. By examining and signing the bill, the payer authorizes the movement of funds to the payee's account.[37]

POINT-OF-SALE TERMINALS

When the concept of a "checkless society" was first introduced, one of its precepts called for the widespread use of computer terminals activated by a bank card. Cardholders presumably would use these to pay for purchases by directly transferring funds to a payee's account. If the consumer insisted on paying by check, the terminal could be designed to

[36]Steve Pastore, "EFT and the Consumer," *The Bankers Magazine*, March-April 1979, p. 39.

[37]George C. White, Jr., "Electronic GIRO or Credit Transfer Payments," *United States Investor*, October 4, 1976, p. 17.

provide a guarantee of payment to the merchant. Under the first option the seller of goods or services would benefit through immediate availability of funds, and the consumer would be spared the expense and inconvenience or issuing a check. Under the second option merchants would no longer have to cope with the chronic problem of bad checks. Point-of-sale (POS) terminals could also be designed to give the store complete inventory controls and sales records.

The magic pieces of plastic that are essential in this system can no longer be referred to as "credit cards," since they are now being used to reduce the cardholder's account balance. Each use of a card to obtain cash from an automated teller machine or to pay a merchant by transfer of funds constitutes a debit to the user's account. Therefore, the term "bank card" is far more valid and appropriate today.

During 1971 and 1972 City National Bank and Trust Company introduced the POS concept in Columbus, Ohio, using sixty terminals in thirty merchant locations. Customers used a bank card containing a magnetic strip, authorizing electronic payments against their accounts. In New York the Hempstead Bank implemented a similar plan in 1971.[38]

However, progress in gaining widespread consumer approval of the POS concept has been disappointingly slow. A survey conduted in 1976 among 800 households disclosed that 30 percent disliked POS, 18 percent were neutral, and only 6 percent strongly favored it. Among the reasons given for opposition were fear of overspending, personal preference for paying by check or cash, and the possibility of computer error.[39]

Perhaps the most controversial and innovative POS use is that which Hinky Dinky, a supermarket chain in Nebraska, introduced in 1974. Terminals in the stores were directly connected to a computer at First Federal Savings and Loan Association, and clients of the latter were given encoded cards that could be presented to a Hinky Dinky clerk to activate the terminal. Shoppers had the option of paying for grocery purchases by direct transfers of funds to Hinky Dinky's account at the savings and loan, depositing funds to a First Federal account, or withdrawing funds. In the last case the clerk would give the shopper cur-

[38]Candilis, op. cit., p. 126.
[39]Olin S. Pugh and Franklin J. Ingram, "EFT and the Public," *The Bankers Magazine*, March-April 1978, p. 47.

rency, and the terminal would perform the same functions as if a purchase had been made.

The Hinky Dinky-First Federal program proved an immediate success. Within 45 days, the savings and loan showed a gain of $603,000 in deposits, of which almost one-half came from new customers. The traditional family trip to the supermarket could now be combined with deposit or withdrawal transactions that would otherwise have necessitated visits to a bank. Hinky Dinky gained through immediate crediting of funds, reduced losses on checks, and expanded sales. The consumer found a convenience in this program that no commercial bank could match.[40]

Bankers were quick to challenge this development. The Nebraska Attorney General and the Nebraska Bankers Association brought litigation against both the savings and loan and the supermaket, charging them with illegal entry into the commercial banking business and infringement of banking functions. State courts ruled in favor of the defendants in both cases.[41]

In addition to its deposit expansion, First Federal found that it had achieved substantial cost reductions each time a deposit or withdrawal was made through the store terminals. Instead of the $1.67 per transation at a teller's window, the Hinky Dinky transaction cost $0.82.[42]

The court ruling in favor of this program gave strong impetus to the Federal Home Loan Bank Board to encourage its savings and loan members to implement similar projects. The nation's fourth largest savings and loan, California Federal, promptly began installation of 200 terminals in supermarkets. Other savings and loan associations have followed this patterm.[43]

Reaction to both the program and the litigation was not confined to Nebraska. Commercial banks voiced immediate concern over the fact that a competing type of financial institution was offering remote terminal facilities that not only handled point-of-sale funds transfers, but also enabled customers to make deposits and withdrawals. In December 1974 James Smith, then Comptroller of the Currency, issued an interpretation of the National Bank Act, allowing all national banks to estab-

[40]"An S & L Puts the Teller in the Supermarket," *Business Week*, April 20, 1974, p. 88.

[41]Alan Richman, "Court Upholds Hinky Dinky EFTS Service," *Bank Systems and Equipment*, September 1974, p. 8.

[42]Louderback, *op. cit.*, p. 48.

[43]"Memphis S and L Goes on Line," *Bank Systems and Equipment*, February 1974. p. 8.

lish customer-bank communication terminals (CBCTs) without regard for state-imposed restrictions on branching.[44] Since this was not a direct regulation but an interpretation of the Act, it became effective immediately upon publication.[45] Its effects, and subsequent developments, are discussed in the final section of this chapter.

The Outlook for POS

From the merchants' standpoint, point-of-sale terminals may prove to be one of the most widely used EFTS applications. Department stores, groceries, furniture stores, and many other retail outlets have been identified as likely candidates for installations, and one study predicts that the number of terminals (approximately 1000 at year-end 1977) will increase to 10,000 in 1985.[46] As with other aspects of EFTS, however, it is the consumer who must make the ultimate decision about the value of the system. Banks that wish to increase customer acceptance of POS must stress the fact that the benefits outweigh the perceived costs, such as computer error or unauthorized use. The dollar amount of a purchase and the type of merchandise being bought may induce a customer to accept the system in one case and reject it in another. For example, the individual who is making a small purchase and leaving the store with it immediately is likely to use a card to pay for the item, whereas the buyer of a major appliance or of furniture will be reluctant to give the merchant immediate use of the funds while the customer himself is waiting for home delivery.

AUTOMATED TELLER MACHINES

Of all actual and potential EFT services, the one with which the average consumer can most easily identify is the automated teller machine (ATM), of which 8000 were in place throughout the country in 1977. One study projects that 125,000 such units will be in place by 1985.[47]

[44]"Off-Premise Teller Ruled Branch in Michigan," *American Banker*, December 12, 1974, p. 2.
[45]12 CFR 7.7491 (1974).
[46]Marc J. Franke, "Self-Service: An Emerging Trend in Retail Banking," *Chase Directions*, New York, The Chase Manhattan Bank, N.A., Fall 1979, p. 2.
[47]*Ibid.*

The ATM represents one area of EFTS in which the predictions of the original visionaries have come to fruition—probably because, with some reservations, consumers have found that it relates must closely to their needs and gives them the convenience of 24-hour banking every day of the year.

In their infancy these machines were far simpler and were commonly referred to as "cash dispensing units." Through use of a bank card, the user could obtain a supply of currency at any time. This eliminated the two-fold consumer problem of drawing a check and waiting in a long line to cash it at a bank. From the bank's standpoint, the ATM similarly solved two problems at the same time. If these units could be operated at points remote from the bank itself, they could replace branch facilities, which were proving less profitable as rent and staff expenses increased.[48] In addition, the ATMs would reduce customer traffic at the remaining branches.

Some banks have placed their ATMs "on line" by connecting them directly to a central computer, so that every transaction is immediately posted to an account. In other cases the ATM merely produces a record of all activity, which is posted at the close of business.

The original simple cash dispending unit has been replaced by far more sophisticated equipment justifying the title of "automated teller." These machines can be used not only to supply cash, but also to initiate transfers among accounts, accept deposits, and receive loan payments. Tests are being conducted to determine the feasibility of using ATMs to dispense traveler's checks at banks, in direct competition with a similar terminal program already implemented by American Express.[49] Such ATMs typically cost $35,000 or more, exclusive of any expenses incurred in building special quarters to house them. This expense has led banks to explore the idea of shared terminals, so that a single unit can access the computer files of several affiliated financial institutions. The National Commission on Electronic Funds Transfers recommended that legislation be enacted wherever necessary to permit such sharing; the New York State Bankers have seconded this[50]; and the amendments

[48]Bank labor costs are said to be increasing at 8 percent per year, See Roger J. Abouchar, "EFT is Inexorable," *American Banker*, May 22, 1979, p. 4.

[49]"Citibank Tests Dispensing of Traveler's Checks at an ATM," *American Banker*, October 31, 1979.

[50]"Comments on the Recommendations of the NCEFT," New York State Bankers Association, April 1978, pp. 31-32

made in 1979 to Regulation E of the Federal Reserve permitted two or more banks or other financial institutions to contract with one another for this purpose.[51]

The fundamental question of ATM placement has become a major problem ever since the Comptroller of the Currency published his 1974 interpretation of the statutes. In many cases banks have installed ATMs as direct physical adjuncts to their premises, so that no legal question arises. It is in the other, far more numerous situations that controversy and litigation have surfaced. The bank that contemplates introducing ATMs or expanding its existing ATM network can choose from the models produced by eight different manufacturers; when it selects the most modern unit, it is purchasing what is known as a CBCT, and must consider all the constraints that may apply.

A recent study not only analyzes the demographics of existing users of ATMs, but also provides useful data for future marketing programs.[52] Of the respondents who made deposits through ATMs, 78.6 percent were younger than 35, and 57.2 percent had incomes of $10,500 or more. Of those who used ATMs to obtain cash, 60 percent were under 35 and 60 percent had incomes of $10,500 or more. Sixty percent of the American populace now lives in suburban areas—the same areas where supermarkets abound. May banks install ATMs in these stores to serve existing depositors and attract new ones? To the supermarket operators the prospect is extremely appealing. Even if the proposed ATMs do not have the capability to charge customers' purchases to accounts, as at Hinky Dinky, they can supply cash and thus lessen check usage.[53] Would installing ATMs in department stores, airports, and other heavily frequented locations serve the interests of bank customers and generate the volume increases necessary to offset the equipment costs? What is the legal status and actual definition of a CBCT that is geographically remote from the bank or banks that own or share it?

Each of these questions has been addressed by federal and/or state regulators, and the banker who seeks a unanimity of answers is doomed to frustrating disappointment. There is little agreement, even among

[51] "Electronic Funds Transfers," Federal Reserve Bank of the New York, Circular 8669, October 29, 1979.

[52] Jerry M. Hood, "Demographics of ATMs," *The Bankers Magazine*, November-December 1979, p. 69.

[53] Almost 80 percent of supermarket sales of $90 billion are paid for by check (Louderback, *op. cit.*, p. 47).

judicial bodies. The reasons for this reflect a long-standing lack of uniformity in matters concerning the regulation of banking, even in so basic an area as defining "branch."[54]

The McFadden Act of 1927 is the fundamental law affecting the ability of any national bank to open new branches. It provides that they may do so *only* to the extent that state-chartered banks have the identical privilege; if state laws restrict or prohibit branching, national banks are bound equally by those statutes. Section 36(f) of the Act defines a branch as "any bank office, agency, or place of business where deposits are received, checks paid, or money lent.[55] By a 6 to 2 vote, the Supreme Court reinforced this Act in 1969 and stated that offering any of the three abovementioned services at any location would constitute *prima facie* evidence of branch banking.[56]

The Comptroller's interpretation of the Act in 1974 addressed the question of CBCTs as branches of national banks and concluded that CBCTs should not be restricted in the same fashion as brick-and-mortar branches. Obviously, CBCTs had not been contemplated when federal laws on branching were originally passed. It was the Comptroller's opinion that CBCTs were not bound by the statutes, and that a national bank could therefore install these facilities anywhere.

It must be noted that the Comptroller was trying to place national banks on the same competitive basis as savings and loan associations and credit unions, which were not bound by the McFadden provision. The incumbent Comptroller has expressed his personal agreement with his predecessor's interpretation and has spoken in support of Congressional revision of the Act.[57]

Predictably, a storm of controversy was touched off by the 1974 interpretation. Numerous challenges were brought by various groups, including associations of banks who claimed that the Comptroller had violated federal laws; these associations therefore initiated litigation against him. Michigan's Commissioner of Financial Institutions immediately issued a ruling contrary to the Comptroller's, stating that CBCTs were to be considered as branches and were subject to the state's regulations on

[54]"What is Branch Banking?," *Datamation*, February 1975, p. 81.
[55]12 U.S.C., Section 36.
[56]396 U.S. 135.
[57]John G. Heimann with Richard B. Miller, "A Conversation with the Comptroller," *The Bankers Magazine*, January-February 1979, pp. 28–29.

branching.[58] A federal moratorium on all CBCT expansion was called for in a bill introduced in Congress. Two federal district courts, in adjudicating lawsuits brought against the Comptroller, ruled in his favor; subsequently, four U.S. Courts of Appeals, in separate decisions, ruled to the contrary, and the Comptroller was ordered to rescind his original interpretation.[59]

The controversy is by no means completely settled. The decisions by the Courts of Appeals are taken to mean that CBCTs *are* subject to state laws on branching *if* the states categorize them as branches. If so, all CBCT installations must meet the same capital requirements that the states impose for brick-and-mortar branches.[60] At this time, the statutes of eighteen states declare that CBCTs are not branches, while six maintain that they are. New Mexico has classified unmanned terminals as bank branches, but feels that manned facilities (e.g., POS terminals) are not. Delaware's State Bank Commissioner is supporting a bill that will classify all off-premises EFT devices as branches. Other states still have the question under review.[61]

At present, thirty-one states have authorized banks to offer EFT services, and efforts to enact similar laws are under way in other states. For the most part, the statutes that permit banks to enter the EFTS field define and limit the services that may be offered. This is especially true with regard to remote terminal facilities.

Through this bewildering succession of judicial and regulatory rulings and interpretations, some of which reversed earlier decisions, the question of states' rights has consistently surfaced, and the authority of each state to regulate *all* forms of branching within its borders has been reinforced in every case. If any confusion appears to exist about the fact that the specifics of state laws on the whole subject of EFT differ from one state to another, it must be tempered by the realization that the traditional principle of separation of powers, as between the federal and state governments, still prevails. A uniform banking policy throughout the nation, standardizing the EFTS program and declared by a single cen-

[58]"Off-Premise Teller Ruled Branch in Michigan," *American Banker*, December 12 1974, p. 1.

[59]40 Federal Register 49077 (1975).

[60]John G. Heimann in "Banking in Transition," *The Bankers Magazine*, September-October 1978, p. 22.

[61]New Mexico is a "limited branching" state; Delaware allows unlimited statewide branch banking.

tral authority, may not be appropriate to address the community needs in each of the fifty states; any attempt by a federal regulatory agency to do so would certainly provoke a new series of lawsuits and a new area of controversy. Of far more importance at this time is the ability of commercial banks to act, to the extent permitted by state laws, to meet the increasing and intense competition of those institutions that are not bound by the same laws.

INTERBANK EFT NETWORKS

To facilitate the movement of funds from bank to bank, two specialized EFT systems have been developed. They are cited here as examples of the initiative taken by the private sector in developing improved facilities for funds transfers.

CHIPS is the acronym for Clearing House Interbank Payments System. It was formed by the Clearing House member banks in New York City in 1970 and is used only for direct transfers of funds, typically in very large amounts, among its seventy-three participants. It is currently handling over 35,000 messages per day, resulting in an average daily volume of over $70 billion. Transactions are initiated in a rigid data format and are settled through electronic debits and credits to the accounts at the New York Fed of the eleven member banks in the Clearing House.

SWIFT is the acronym for Society of Worldwide Interbank Financial Telecommunications. It does not handle funds settlements but processes instructions, using numerical data field codes, for third party transfers, foreign exchange, and letters of credit. It was implemented in 1977 through agreements among North American and European bank representatives.

The Fed recently announced an experimental program, aimed at speeding and improving the clearing of large-dollar checks through a variation of EFTS. By way of illustration, the Fed assumes that a check for $100,000 or more was sent by a Minneapolis corporation to an Atlanta vendor. The check is deposited in a bank in Atlanta. That bank converts the payment instructions to magnetic tape and follows the same procedure for all large checks received on that day. Tapes from all the Atlanta banks are then delivered to the Atlanta Fed, which sorts the payment instructions by destination and sends them to the Federal Reserve Banks in each of the twelve districts. The latter then instruct the drawee banks to create account debits.[62]

THE STATE OF THE ART

Paul Nadler[63] has described the early forecasts of a "checkless society" and the projections of quick, widespread acceptance of all forms of EFTS as "vastly exaggerated." A great deal of progress has indeed been made in many areas of EFTS implementation, but much unforeseen resistance has also been encountered. It is now apparent that the prophets ignored a basic truth: consumers and users, and not new technology, drive the market.

The potential benefits to many categories of EFTS users still exist. Corporations can no doubt gain quicker availability of funds, more accurate and complete data on payments received and disbursed, and savings in postage and handling costs. Yet questions of float reduction and reciprocity arise. The corporate treasurer may be willing to adopt a system that allows him to receive funds more quickly, but will not consider one that draws down his bank balances with the same speed. He must also wonder if his counterparts at other firms will handle transactions involving his company in the same manner.

There is no doubt that employees can benefit through direct deposit of payroll. Check cashing costs and problems, and losses and thefts of salary checks, can be completely or partially eliminated. Yet many employees continue to insist on cash or check payments. They do not consider check cashing to be a problem and fear a loss of personal privacy. Similarly, their employers, who would also stand to gain substantially through direct deposit, cite the loss of float or the lack of demonstrated bottom-line benefits as the main reasons for opposing it.

There is no doubt that paying bills through EFTS can, in certain cases, be advantageous to both remitter and recipient. Yet, again, consumers have expressed strong reservations. The fear that a "big brother" is gathering and reporting all their personal financial transactions

[62]"Electronic Presentment of Checks," Federal Reserve Bank of New York, Circular 8573, May 17, 1979.

[63]In "Banking: The Next Ten Years," *The Bankers Magazine*, July-August 1978, p. 56.

[64]Nadler, "*The Human Side of Electronic Banking*," p. 14.

through a computer is pervasive.[64] Other individuals mention fears of computer malfunction, fears a payment will not be processed in a timely manner, and fears of not having receipts to document every transaction.[65]

There is no doubt that ATMs offer the maximum convenience to depositors. ATMs are accessible at all times and eliminate at least part of the volume that causes long lines at tellers' windows. Under proper security conditions "push-button" banking ought to have far more appeal than issuing and cashing checks.

Thousands of bank customers appreciate these advantages and use ATMs. In the New York area, Citibank invested some $200 million in a comprehensive ATM plan for its 271 branches[66] and has found that 68 percent of its withdrawals of funds are made through these units.[67] Similar successes have been reported by banks in Georgia, Pennsylvania, and Florida, and at some ATMs transaction volume has reached a monthly level of 50,000.[68]

Yet many other consumers refuse to use ATMs. The study by Pugh and Ingram[69] of 800 households indicated that 42 percent considered ATMs "not needed." Again fears were expressed: fears that unauthorized persons might have access to accounts, fears of being robbed after having obtained cash from an ATM, and fears of computer errors.

As the original, basic cash dispensing unit evolved into a CBCT capable of handling many other types of transactions, it was logical to predict that consumer usage would increase. Unfortunately this projected success has not occurred as quickly or as extentively as was called for by the original scenario. If commercial banks had been granted the same CBCT latitude enjoyed by their competitors, the results might well have been different; but the plethora of rulings, decisions, and state laws has served only to create a climate in which savings and loan associations, credit unions, and major financially oriented companies such as Sears Roebuck operate at a real advantage.

If the total experience of commercial banks with all forms of private-sector EFTS (excluding the federal goverment's programs) were to be analyzed, one basic theme could be developed: the future of EFTS

[65]Candilis, *op. cit.*, p. 129.
[66]"Citibank's New Automated Banking," *Forbes*, March 6, 1978, pp. 84-87.
[67]Steven Pastore, "EFT and the Consumer," p. 37.
[68]Louderback, *op. cit.*, p. 48.
[69]*Op. cit.*, p. 45.

depends not on new technology (for that is already in place), but on concerted efforts by bankers to educate the public regarding the potential benefits of the system. Executive Vice President John Lee of the New York Clearing House Association has called for a two-way communication process, in which the banks will listen to consumer views about what is actually needed and wanted, and consumers will listen to bankers' views and explanations. The message must be conveyed that EFTS programs have not been designed purely for the banks' profit purposes.[70]

Customer acceptance of EFTS can be achieved only through an educational program that dispels the fears and reservations so frequently expressed by so many categories of potential EFTS users. A "less-check" rather than a "checkless" society *is* possible, but it cannot be force-fed to a public that does not fully understand it and in many cases sees no good reason for helping it to arrive[71]

[70]"The Automated Clearing House Network: Its Progress, Problems, Potential," *Banking*, March 1979, p. 84. This article also presents the views of Federal Reserve and industry experts on many EFTS-related topics.

[71]Nadler, in "Banking in Transition," *The Bankers Magazine*, September-October 1978, p. 28.

VIII

MULTINATIONAL BANKING

During his unsuccessful campaign for the United States presidency in 1940, Wendell Willkie espoused the concept of "One World" and published a book bearing that title. His basic thinking was that nations were actually interdependent, and that the actions of any major power inevitably affected all the others, regardless of the geographical distances separating them. Willkie's ideas surprised and alienated many Americans, whose attitudes were far more parochial and narrow. In 1940 America's gross national product had recovered from the depression, and the average individual's standard of living was far better than that of his or her counterparts in other countries. Hence the prevailing feeling was that the United States need not become involved with foreign nations and could very well exist alone, untroubled by the problems of others and indifferent to any marketing opportunities that other countries might offer. This feeling was articulated on the floor of Congress by leaders of the isolationist movement and was implicit in the actions of banking and business leaders, who chose to operate outside the United States only on a limited basis.

Willkie's notion of the interdependence of all nations and his predictions of vastly expanded foreign trade for America supply a prelude to one of the major changes in our banking history. Traditional barriers and philosophical objections vanished as American banks began to move into every corner of the world. Foreign banks subsequently followed the same course of action and became a major force in our overall financial and economic picture. Were he still alive, Willkie might be gratified to see his wish and prophecy realized in the tremendous volume of transactions that are now processed each day under the generic heading of international banking.

The end of World War II was followed by the gradual rebuilding of the shattered economies of many countries, accompanied by a natural increase in demand for many products by the populations of those countries. Their own manufacturers' facilities had, in many cases, been destroyed during the war; therefore, they turned to America to supply the goods they needed. American corporations, identifying these new markets, began introducing their products into nations throughout the world. American chemical products were sold to German farmers; American food products began to appear on the shelves of British and French grocery stores; American cash registers and computers were sold to merchants and industrialists in many countries; and American exports assumed greater importance in our economy.

Many of those same American corporations found that they could obtain relatively inexpensive labor and raw materials outside the United States. Others needed imports of essential goods to manufacture their products. Foreign factories, distribution points, and import offices were opened to handle all phases of trade, and the names of America's industrial giants became as well known in Europe and the Far East as in the United States.

FOREIGN OPERATIONS OF U.S. BANKS

The expansion of American business abroad led commercial banks to perceive the wisdom of following the lead of their major corporate clients in identifying new markets and establishing overseas facilities. In steadily increasing numbers throughout the postwar years, they abandoned their isolationism and parochial attitudes and adopted a policy of following their customers. Wherever a corporation from the "Fortune 500" list was functioning, an American commercial bank sought the approval of the local government to open a branch or otherwise establish a presence. In 1947 only seven American banks had opened foreign branches[1]; by 1970 sixty-one U.S. banks had foreign offices that held

[1]Martin Mayer, *The Bankers*, New York, David McKay Co., 1974, p. 437.

$50 billion in assets, and by the end of 1978 155 American banks had foreign-office assets of $260 billion.[2]

In the 20 years following the cessation of hostilities in World War II, short-term loans made by American banks to foreign borrowers increased almost 900 percent.[3] A recent study of ten of the largest U.S. banks showed international contributions to their net earnings of 51 percent in 1977 and 46 percent in 1978.[4]

The most important traditional components of foreign banking business continue, including loans, letters of credit, money transfers, collections of drafts and other instruments, foreign exchange, and trust receipt financing; in many cases, they have been supplemented by new services, but it is their sheer volume that is chiefly responsible for the growth in transactions and earnings.

The world's economies have become increasingly interdependent. Any OPEC increase is felt throughout the global economy. Japan, Germany, and many smaller countries depend heavily on foreign trade, and the emergence of new nations and the expansion of currency trading have combined with this to create opportunities for banks to provide services to a far broader range of customers.

American banks today participate in syndicates that extend large foreign credits. They penetrate the Iron Curtain by opening branches in countries that for years were sealed off from the Western world. They establish local facilities to provide installment loans and checking and savings accounts to consumers. They operate foreign subsidiaries engaged in various types of leasing. They have assumed a leading role as direct lenders to foreign governments. Their networks of "offshore" banking centers provide them with tax and operational-cost advantages and permit them to function under prevailing liberal regulations imposed by a local government.

Claims on foreigners of foreign branches of U.S. banks have grown at an annual rate of 33 percent since 1969, and gross Eurocurrency depos-

[2]Barbara Negris, "Insured Commercial Bank Income in 1978," *Federal Reserve Bulletin*, September 1979, p. 701.

[3]Frederick Heldring, "The International Banking Function of U.S. Commercial Banks," in Herbert V. Prochnow and Herbert V. Prochnow, Jr. (Eds.), *The Changing World of Banking*, New York, Harper & Row, 1974, p. 347.

[4]L. Michael Cacace, "100 Top-Earning Bank Firms Set Record," *American Banker*, April 2, 1979, p. 1.

its of major American banks have increased from $57 billion in 1969 to $448 billion in 1978.[5]

EUROCURRENCIES

The entire concept of funds management has taken on new dimensions through the Eurodollar—an entry in U.S. dollars on the books of a foreign bank or overseas branch of an American bank. The reasons for the growth of Eurodollars may be understood through an analogy that compares the position of the American dollar in world trade in recent years with that of the bank notes that proliferated in the United States before 1863.

In theory the bank notes were redeemable in specie if presented to the issuer; similarly, dollars had value in terms of their potential convertibility to gold. In actual practice, of course, an issuing bank never had sufficient specie to permit conversion of all its notes at one time, and the United States did not have enough gold to redeem all outstanding dollars. The essential element in each case is simply a faith in the soundness of the paper money.

If a major American corporation earns $10 million on European sales and deposits the funds in the London branch of a U.S. bank, the money becomes loanable by that bank in any part of the world, but it is not subject to the reserve requirements of the Fed or other regulatory agencies. This freedom from reserves lowers the bank's costs; hence it can pay a higher rate of interest on funds and can lend those funds out at lower rates.

When America in the 1960s followed the pattern set by Great Britain in the 1950s and attempted to improve its balance of payments position by forbidding companies to export dollars to build foreign plants, companies reacted by using Eurodollars as their source of funds. When OPEC announced its price increases in 1973 and 1974, its members, unable to spend their new profits quickly enough, simply deposited funds with banks outside the United States. These two historical developments supply much of the background for the growth of Eurodollars. The continued American deficit in balance of payments led to devalu-

[5]Warren E. Moskowitz, "Global Asset and Liability Management at Commercial Banks," Federal Reserve Bank of New York, *Quarterly Review*, Spring 1979, pp. 45-46.

ations of the U.S. dollar in 1971 and 1973 and a suspension of the dollar's convertibility into gold at any price. Therefore, the holders of dollars sought ways to put them to profitable use in lieu of actual conversion, further fueling the Eurodollar expansion.[6]

Eurodollars today are used to purchase profitable and liquid instruments in the money market, and are loaned directly to banks in the United States so that the latter, in turn, can accomodate their own customers. In 1970 the liabilities of major U.S. commercial banks to their foreign branches averaged $13 billion. By 1974, when American banks experienced one of the most severe "credit crunch" cycles in history, the figure had grown to $270 billion, and banks were paying rates as high as 13 percent for Eurodollars.

The operation of a network of foreign branches obviously permits a bank to serve the needs of its multinational customers anywhere in the world. The Eurodollar is a major component in this flexibility, since these funds are readily available and provide the mechanism whereby OPEC nations "recycle" their new wealth to other countries. Funds management, for many major banks today, has become largely dependent on global communications. If the current status of each foreign branch is known to all the others, funds can easily be moved and one branch can borrow from another instead of using the open market at a higher rate.

RISK AND RELATED FACTORS

The keystone of international operations at major banks is the financing of foreign trade, chiefly through direct loans or letters of credit. Second in overall importance is the extension of credit to correspondent banks overseas. The third area involves direct lending to foreign governments, and it is this particular facet of international banking that is creating great concern at the present time.

Global lending must necessarily take into account a dimension of risk that is absent in domestic banking: the economic stability of the country in which loans are being made. The risk factors in making loans to a firm in, or the government of, a particular nation include political and

[6]Mayer, *op. cit.*, p. 451.

economic conditions demanding careful analysis. There are three contemporary situations that are extremely relevant.

As part of their overall approach to the social responsibility of banks, stockholders have subjected some of America's largest financial institutions to questions regarding the desirability and extent of loans made in South Africa and Chile. It is the shareholders' contention that the banks should play no part in helping companies to function in those countries where violations of civil rights are alleged to take place. As a gesture of protest, institutional and individual stockholders have sold their shares in some of the major commercial banks and have publicized this severing of their investment ties. In rebuttal the banks in question have pointed out that their credit facilities are not being provided to support the local government, nor have they taken a position in support of a government's policies. Rather, they have simply assessed a borrowing customer's creditworthiness and approved a loan without using geography as a criterion.

The second contemporary topic reflects the banks' concern over possible revolutions in foreign counties where loan and investment exposure exists. There is substantial historical evidence of losses incurred by banks as a direct result of changes in government; a new regime in a country may arbitrarily decide to nationalize banks and industries and to repudiate all outstanding government obligations. This was the pattern followed by Castro in Cuba; all loans incurred by the Batista government were cancelled and all American banking offices on the island were expropriated.[7] Events in Iran in 1979 offer further evidence of the effect on banks of the overthrow of a local government. American bankers must take this fundamental risk into consideration as they assess international loans.

The third area of concern involves some $48.7 billion now owed to U.S. banks by the so-called less-developed countries (LDCs).[8] These less-developed countries account for 24 percent of total foreign commercial loan outstandings of U.S. banks, and Henry Reuss, Chairman of the House Banking Committee, has been severely critical of the manner in which banks have continued to lend in and to LDCs despite adverse indicators.

[7]Frederick Heldring, "The International Banking Function of U.S. Commercial Banks," Prochnow and Prochnow, *op. cit.*, p. 351.

[8]"A Threat to Global Growth," *Time*, July 2, 1979, pp. 54–55.

Concern over the repayment abilities of the LDCs has steadily mounted as oil price increases and other economic pressures have affected their financial structures. Total external debts of LDCs to all lenders now exceed $205 billion, according to the Organization for Economic Cooperation and Development, and have been escalating at an annual rate of 15 percent.[9] There are valid questions as to whether loans to such countries should be curtailed, and, as pressures increase on banks to limit their exposure, investors tend to take a dim view of the entire situation; market values for bank stocks decline accordingly.

The nation of Zaire particularly has been singled out as a prototype of the LDC problem. Its government's external debt is now believed to total $3.5 billion, including a syndicated loan of $215 million and a single loan of $40 million made directly to the government by a U.S. bank.[10]

Loans were also made to corporations that were anxious to exploit Zaire's mineral riches. However, the nation's economy was adversely affected by local insurrections and falling copper prices, and the future stability of the government has been questioned. The repayment of these private-sector credits may also pose a serious problem.

In 1974 the Fed, alarmed over the continued expansion of overseas lending, strongly recommended that American banks slow their rate of growth in this area.[11] As a result, risk factors may now receive more attention than in the past; yet foreign loans increased 12 percent in 1978 and have reached a figure of $217 billion.[12]

Formal state bankruptcies are not necessarily expected, but it appears almost certain that lending banks will be confronted with requests for moratoriums or some form of refinancing.[13]

Analysis of Country Risk

Although American banks' domestic operations are, almost without exception, subject to control by one or more agencies of the federal govern-

[9]"Default Threatens Those LDC Loans Again," *Business Week*, July 2, 1979, p. 79.

[10]Michael Quint, "A Bleak Outlook for Troubled Zaire," *American Banker*, April 9, 1979, p. 1.

[11]Joseph D. Hutynan, "Fed for First Time Denies Expansion," *American Banker*, September 12, 1974, p. 1.

[12]Anthony E. Mattera, "U.S. Bank Claims on Foreigners Rose 12%," *American Banker*, June 25, 1979, p. 3.

[13]Henry Simon Bloch, "Foreign Risk Judgment for Commercial Banks," *The Bankers Magazine*, Autumn 1977, p. 92.

ment, the same does not hold true in their foreign operations. A bank, for example, is limited in the unsecured amount it can lend to any one borrower in the United States, but no such limit exists on the amount it can lend in the public and private sectors within the borders of any foreign country. Even for loans to foreign governments more than one agency may borrow, thus creating a single debt far beyond the amount that a bank could lend to one of the largest U.S. corporations.

Federal authorities have recommended a more thorough and systematic approach to the supervision of international banking, and the office of the Comptroller of the Currency now uses a risk report that identifies concentrations of lending in a particular country.[14]

To minimize risk in the foreign loan portfolio, various forms of specialized analysis may be employed. These include detailed approaches to the international, political, economic, and sociocultural factors that can be identified in a country and can be used to develop a rating scale that classifies risk.[15] They can also be refined to provide guidelines for both short- and long-term lending, interest rates, and the limits that appear appropriate for both private-sector and public-sector loans.[16]

FOREIGN EXCHANGE OPERATIONS

A Senior Vice President of the New York Fed has described foreign exchange trading as "probably one of the most widely discussed and yet least understood subjects of our times."[17] His reference is to an area where billions of dollars change hands every day, and banks and customers function under intense pressures and assume high risks. Rumors, heightened tensions among nations, political sensitivities, and economic predictions affect each day's operations. Still fresh in the minds of many bankers, is 1974, a year in which the Franklin National Bank and Bankhaus Herstatt collapsed, and Union Bank (Switzerland) and Lloyds Bank (England) admitted tens of millions of dollars in losses—all caused

[14]A New Supervisory Approach to Foreign Lending," Federal Reserve Bank of New York, *Quarterly Review*, Spring 1978, pp. 1-6.

[15]Tracy G. Herrick, *Bank Analyst's Handbook*, New York, Wiley, 1978, pp. 242-243.

[16]Christopher M. Korth, "Developing a Country-Risk Analysis System," *The Journal of Commercial Bank Lending*, December 1979, pp. 56-57.

[17]Scott E. Pardee, "How Well Are the Exchange Markets Functioning?," Federal Reserve Bank of New York, *Quarterly Review*, Spring 1979, p. 49.

entirely or in part by foreign exchange trades.[18] Yet the possibility of substantial profits is as ever-present as the risk factor.

The dollar was more vulnerable in the foreign exchange market in 1978. By October it had dropped 36 percent in value against the yen, 35 percent against the Swiss franc, and 22 percent against the German mark.[19] These declines threatened to throw the entire international financial system into disarray. Accordingly, a series of actions, including provision for up to $30 billion of additional resources, was taken by President James Earl Carter and officials of both the Treasury Department and Federal Reserve to correct the situation.[20]

An analysis of the data furnished by three of the major New York Clearing House banks discloses their ability to benefit from the increase in transaction volume and the currency fluctuations that took place in 1978. At Chemical Bank foreign exchange trading profits were 190 percent higher than in 1977; at Bankers Trust 79 percent higher; and at Chase Manhattan 54 percent higher.[21]

However, banks cannot depend on federal government intervention to insure the profitability of their foreign exchange trading operations, nor should they continually look to Washington to bolster the market. Prudence and maximum use of forecasting techniques and other data are indispensable in this field, and the onus is on the banks to protect themselves as completely as possible.

EDGE ACT FACILITIES

In 1919 Congress passed the Edge Act as an amendment to the Federal Reserve Act, and the provisions of the former were later incorporated into the latter under Regulation K. However, it was only in the years following World War II that American banks began to take full advantage of it, and since that time it has enabled them to broaden the scope of their international operations in many ways.

[18]Mayer, *op. cit.*, pp. 476–477.

[19]"Monetary Policy and Open Market Operations in 1978," Federal Reserve Bank of New York, *Quarterly Review*, Spring 1979, p. 64.

[20]Alan R. Holmes and Scott E. Pardee, "Treasury and Federal Reserve Foreign Exchange Operations," Federal Reserve Bank of New York, *Quarterly Review*, Spring 1979, pp. 67–68.

[21]Annual Report, 1978.

The Edge Act allows commercial banks to cross state lines to open specialized offices that are not allowed to handle any purely domestic business. These offices can assist customers with all types of international banking transactions. Because so much of our foreign trade originates in San Francisco, Chicago, Miami, and Houston, these cities have become the favored locations for Edge Act offices. The act also allows banks to form subsidiaries that can acquire minority or controlling interests in foreign banks, and to establish overseas operations for investment and mortgage banking, leasing, factoring, and consumer financing.

THE FOREIGN BANKS

There is a striking and exact corollary between the pattern of international growth in American industry and banking and that of foreign businesses and banks. As was noted earlier, many of America's major corporations recognized the potential of the overseas markets in the years following World War II, and the products of IBM, General Foods, Procter and Gamble, Eastman Kodak, and National Cash Register were made available throughout the free would. As these corporations became global in the scope of their operations, American banks emulated them and established strong presences abroad. While preserving their traditional correspondent relationships with foreign banks, they also embarked on a program of overseas branch expansion. New service areas were also devised and implemented to serve the needs of global customers.

Mirroring that growth, an identical evolutionary sequence took place in the opposite direction. Corporations from many foreign countries came first, as exports became vitally necessary to the economic recovery of countries that had experienced the ravages of World War II. America came to represent one of the most fertile markets for many types of foreign merchandise, and in steadily increasing proportions the U.S. deficit in annual balance of payments grew as the nation became a net importer of goods rather than an exporter. Japan, West Germany, Italy, France, and other nations supplied the electronic goods, steel, apparel, and automobiles that American consumers wanted. The low costs of labor and raw materials outside the United States enabled importers to sell at prices below those charged by domestic manufacturers. The OPEC cartel only exacerbated an already troublesome condition.

The growth of foreign trade in the United States was followed by an influx of foreign banks. Just as the American banks had increased their penetration of overseas markets after major industrial firms had taken the lead, so their counterpart banks from other nations expanded their own global operations and became steadily more important in the American economic picture. They accomplished this not only through a concerted effort to deal effectively with their own corporate customers and meet their needs in the United States, but also by capitalizing on a very real competitive advantage.

As recently as 1972 America dominated the world of commercial banking. Four of the ten largest banks, and seventeen of the fifty largest, were American; but by 1978 these figures had shifted dramatically, and only four of the world's thirty largest banks, and seven of the fifty largest, were American.[22] In May 1979 144 foreign banks were operating 315 offices of various types in the United States, up from only 111 offices 6 years earlier. Their "standard banking assets" (the Federal Reserve term for total assets minus claims on related institutions and assets arising in the payments-clearing process) were $97 billion, a figure 4½ times as large as that for May 1973.[23]

During 1978 ninety foreign banks opened one or more offices in the United States; twenty-four of these established a presence here for the first time. This brought to 278 the number of foreign banks represented in America by full-scale branches, representative offices, agencies, subsidiaries, or affiliates.[24]

For purposes of comparison it may be noted that the total assets of all overseas branches of American banks were $259 billion in May 1978. This is more than 2½ times the assets of all foreign banks in the United States.[25]

Foreign banks operate in the United States through three types of facilities: agencies, branches, and subsidiaries. Agencies and branches may conduct full-scale lending operations, but agencies may not accept deposits. Subsidiary commercial banks are separately chartered institu-

[22] *Bank Stock Quarterly*, October 1978, p. 1.

[23] Sydney J. Key and James M. Brundy, "Implementation of the International Banking Act," *Federal Reserve Bulletin*, October 1979, p. 787.

[24] Anthony F. Mattera, "90 Foreign Banks Established U.S. Offices in 1978," *American Banker*, March 23, 1979, p. 2.

[25] *Bank Stock Quarterly*, October 1978, p. 3.

tions and are subject to various federal laws and regulations. Branches are permitted to issues domestic certificates of deposit; agencies may not do so. Branches of foreign banks account for standard assets, according to Federal Reserve criteria, of over $50 billion, or about one-half of the standard assets of all U.S. offices of foreign banks.[26]

The competitive advantage that has made much of this growth possible lies in the ability of foreign banks to open branches and agencies in more than one state "with relative ease."[27] This privilege has been denied to domestic banks since the McFadden Act was passed in 1927. The freedom enjoyed by foreign banks in this respect, and the fact that their facilities (unlike those of virtually all domestic banks) were supervised only by the licensing state and were not required to maintain reserves with the Fed, created a problem that the U.S. Congress considered for many years before the International Banking Act of 1978 was enacted.

Foreign banks have been increasingly successful in securing a large share of the market for commercial and industrial loans in the United States. Their total outstandings under this heading were $27 billion in 1978, a figure that is 20 percent of the total for all major reporting domestic banks and is more than double the showing in 1972 for the same foreign banks.[28]

The extent to which foreign banks have succeeded in penetrating the American market is reflective of the innate ties they have to corporations with which they have close relationships at home. Just as a major U.S. firm operating in Venezuela is likely to do business with the Caracas branch of the American bank to which it is most closely associated, a Japanese bank in San Francisco enjoys a natural marketing advantage when it solicits business from the subsidiary of a corporation headquartered in Tokyo. In making short-term credit available to such companies, the foreign banks have enjoyed considerable success. They have also been able to stress the fact that they can exert influence in their home countries and thus assist American companies that are attempting to expand overseas.[29]

[26]Key and Brundy, *op. cit.*, p. 78.
[27]*Ibid.* (emphasis added).
[28]*Bank Stock Quarterly*, October 1978, p. 3.
[29]"Foreign Banking in America," *Institutional Investor*, September 1977, p. 103.

THE INTERNATIONAL BANKING ACT

In growing numbers and with increased vehemence, American bankers have protested the very significant competitive advantages enjoyed by foreign banks that operate in the United States. The International Banking Act (IBA) of 1978 largely reflects those protests; but the point must be stressed that American bankers did not seek to exclude foreign banks, curtail their right to function, or place them at a competitive disadvantage. Rather, the Act has been described by Key and Brundy as

> part of a general policy of national treatment in order to promote competitive equality between domestic and foreign banking institutions in the United States.[30]

As in the case of EFT services, banks found themselves unable to do what their competitors could do, because of the geographic and statutory limitations that American laws impose. The policy of national treatment attempts to give foreign enterprises the same powers, and to subject them to the same obligations, as their domestic counterparts in host countries.

A bank headquartered in Hong Kong, Amsterdam, or London can cross state lines and/or acquire a New York based bank; domestic commercial banks can do neither. In 1978 there were twenty-seven foreign banks operating in the United States with branches, agencies, or subsidiaries in more than one state.[31] Barclays Bank International, Ltd., led the way, with facilities in New York, Illinois, California, Georgia, Pennsylvania, and Massachusetts. It is baffling to note the liberal posture that some otherwise restrictive states have adopted in this regard. Illinois, for example, continues to prohibit branching within its borders by its own banks, and excludes any branching by other American banks, yet encourages foreign banks to open Illinois offices *and* additional branches. Florida, which traditionally enforced unit banking laws like those of Illinois, has also allowed significant expansion by foreign banks within its state boundaries.

The major provisions of the IBA address this basic question of parity

[30] *Op. cit.*, p. 787.
[31] *Bank Stock Quarterly*, October 1978, p. 6.

of treatment. The Act limits the interstate deposit-taking activities of foreign banks and authorizes the Federal Reserve Board to impose reserve requirements on U.S. agencies and branches of any such bank that has consolidated worldwide assets of $1 billion or more. The Fed was also given power to set the maximum interest rates that agencies and branches of foreign banks may pay on time deposits, thus treating these facilities on the same basis, under Regulation Q, as domestic member banks. The Act made agencies and branches eligible for Federal Reserve services and required those facilities to join FDIC if they were engaged in retail deposit-taking. Edge Act corporations were given more power to compete with agencies and branches.

The Federal Reserve has invited comment from banks and the public on proposed regulatory changes that will implement the provisions of the IBA by incorporating them into Regulation K. In preparing its proposed changes, the Fed has noted that one of the purposes of the IBA was to limit the interstate domestic deposit-taking capabilities of foreign banks. Therefore, a foreign bank with offices in more than one state must choose a "home state" in which it already operates; within that state, it may expand its deposit-taking activities, and beyond it, the bank may open branches or agencies that *do not* accept domestic deposits. Offices that the bank has established in other states may be retained, but new ones may not be added, and no bank in another state may be acquired. Circular 8673 of the Federal Reserve Bank of New York (November 2, 1979) provides these and other details of the revisions to Regulation K.

1979 was a year marked by announcements of large-scale acquisitions of American banks by foreign institutions. One member of the New York Clearing House, National Bank of North America, was purchased by the second largest bank in the United Kingdom, the National Westminster. America's twenty-fifth largest bank, Union Bank (Los Angeles), was bought by Standard Chartered Bank of London, and La Salle National Bank (Chicago) by Algemene Bank Nederland, a $25 billion institution headquartered in Amsterdam. In what was by far the largest of all the acquisitions, Hong Kong and Shanghai Banking Corporation (with total assets of $18.9 billion)took over Marine Midland Bank, which ranks twelfth among all American commercial banks with year-end 1978 assets of $14.3 billion.

The Bankers Trust Company's decision to focus its future attention on wholesale banking was accompanied by an announcement that eighty-nine of its branches were to be sold to Bank of Montreal. When that purchase did not materialize, three other foreign banks—Bank Leumi Trust Company, National Bank of North America (now owned by National Westminster), and Barclays Bank of New York[32]—arranged to purchase fifty-five of the branches.[33]

These acquisitions highlight the fact that existing laws, prior to the passage of the IBA, enabled foreign banks to do what domestic banks could not do. If a major American bank had attempted an acquisition of such magnitude within its own state, a conflict with antitrust laws would immediately be identified and the U.S. Department of Justice would undoubtedly exert every effort to prevent it. If, instead, the proposed acquisition involved a bank holding company in another state, the Bank Holding Company Act of 1956 would be invoked to forestall it.

The issue of reciprocity cannot be ignored in this discussion of foreign bank operations in America. American bankers have not directly sought to exclude foreign banks, prevent them from doing business in the United States, or block the abovementioned acquisitions. Any such action would carry with it the potential for retaliation by a foreign country. The banker who expresses resentment over the acquisition of an American bank by a British buyer must recognize the liberality that has been shown by British banking authorities in allowing American bank branches to proliferate in England, and the same principle applies to other nations. Parity is the key issue.

[32]Barclays Bank International operates two American subsidiaries. Barclays Bank of New York already has thirty-two branches in the New York City area, while its California counterpart has forty-seven in that state.

[33]Robert A. Bennett, "Bankers Trust Sells 55 Branches," *The New York Times*, June 30, 1979, p. D-1.

IX

SPECIALIZED SERVICE AREAS

Under the full service concept, commercial banks in the United States have expanded their horizons and, often with the help of computer technology, moved into specialized areas of customized arrangements that defy classification under other headings. Two of these warrant particular attention. One is traditional, the other relatively new. The *trust services* field dates back to the early days of American banking. The *cash management* family of services began to develop in the 1950s and has shown steady and impressive growth. Both are important components of Full Service banking; and both figure prominently in future planning.

TRUST SERVICES

The fact that so many of the nation's oldest and largest financial institutions include the word "trust" as part of their legal names offers a clue to the history of fiduciary services in America. Many trust companies were organized in the early nineteenth century, often in connection with insurance companies, and operated under state charters to provide investment services. The equities of those who turned their assets over to these trusts resembled shares in an investment fund. By 1850, however, the trust companies had taken on a different character and were accepting demand and time deposits and making short-term loans. This led to resentment among commercial bankers, who found that their competition was coming from entities that operated with minimal supervision and did not have to keep reserves as banks did. Trust companies also enjoyed tax advantages and were able to offer higher interest rates than banks.[1]

To counter this competition, many state-chartered banks sought and obtained trust powers. At the same time, trusts were mushrooming outside banking circles through the formation of various corporate "pools," designed to control the distribution of iron, steel, petroleum, and other goods. The Standard Oil Company trust (1879) served as a prototype. Monopolistic practices, engaged in by some of these trusts, led to federal legislation (the Clayton and Sherman Antitrust Acts) aimed against them.

Fiduciary functions, provided for individual and corporate customers, combined with commercial banking proved highly successful for state-chartered banks. The growth of the trust area as an adjunct to other commercial bank functions received further impetus through the Federal Reserve Act passed in 1913. Section 11 (K) of that Act permitted national banks, for the first time, to apply to federal regulatory agencies for trust powers, but stipulated that such banks would also be subject to the restrictions that any state might impose.[2]

Since 1913 the fiduciary functions of banks have increased tremendously in scope and importance, and over 4000 banks now offer some or all trust services—personal, corporate, or a combination of both.[3] They act as administrators and executors of estates for individuals; provide safekeeping, custody, escrow, and managing agent services; act as registrars, transfer agents, dividend disbursing agents, and trustees under indenture for corporations; and manage pension, profit-sharing, and individual retirement accounts. They are considered to be America's most important single fiduciary group.[4] At year-end 1978, the market value of the trust assets over which banks exercised investment discretion was

[1] Margaret G. Myers, *A Financial History of the United States*, Columbia University Press, 1970, p. 249.

[2] American Bankers Association, *The Commercial Banking Industry*, Englewood Cliffs, NJ, Prentice-Hall, 1962, pp. 297-298.

[3] Martin Mayer, *The Bankers*, New York, David McKay Co., 1974, p. 493.

[4] Howard D. Crosse and George H. Hempel, *Management Policies for Commercial Banks*, Englewood Cliffs, NJ, Prentice-Hall, 1973, p. 9.

over $279 billion; if the values of all other properties entrusted to them on a nondiscretionary basis were to be included, the figure would be very much higher.[5]

Of the aforementioned $279 billion, the five largest banks in the trust field (Morgan Guaranty, Citibank, Bankers Trust, Mellon National, and Harris Trust) alone held $82 billion and reported earnings of $305 million from trust operations in 1978, or an average 3.7 percent of their net operating income.[6]

Competition in the fiduciary-services area is intense and, again, is often provided by organizations that are not subject to the restrictions applied to the commercial banks. Trust operations of the latter are constrained in many ways. Before they can offer any trust services, banks must obtain specific federal and/or state approval and meet capital requirements. At member banks, Federal Reserve Regulation F applies to trust performance and policies. Each bank's trust department is subject to federal and/or state annual examination and must also receive internal audits under the supervision of a Trust Committee of the directors. Any bank wishing to engage in trust operations must pledge specific securities as a means of protecting the assets under its control.[7]

In addition, regulations of the Internal Revenue Service, Securities and Exchange Commission, and Federal Reserve (in the case of bank holding companies) apply to various aspects of trust services.[8] The insurance companies, brokerage houses, law firms, and investment management and estate planning firms that compete with banks for trust business do not have to contend with this set of restrictions.

One relatively new, yet profitable and growing area of trust services came into being when Congress enacted legislation (the Keogh Act and subsequent amendments) allowing self-employed individuals and those not covered by pension plans to set aside money each year toward retirement. Thrift institutions are the commercial banks' major competitors in this area.

[5] "The 50 Largest Trust Operations," *Forbes*, April 16, 1979, p. 135.

[6] *Ibid.*

[7] American Bankers Association, *op cit.*, p. 299.

[8] A comprehensive listing may be found in Herbert V. Prochnow and Herbert V. Prochnow, Jr. (Eds.), *The Changing World of Banking*, New York, Harper & Row, 1974, pp. 207-208.

Trust Marketing

The fundamental concepts of planning can be applied to the trust field to ensure that the appropriate services are being marketed in the right areas. Each bank should determine its present status versus the competition. The latter should be evaluated both quantitatively and qualitatively. Demographic studies can be performed or obtained to show age groups and personal-income concentrations in a community. Publicly held corporations must announce each pension or profit-sharing plan they implement; this publicity can help shape the bank's trust marketing effort. The number of estate tax returns filed in a community each year is a matter of public record and provides some indication of the potential market for such services as estate planning and investment management.

Trust marketing may be conditioned by pricing factors. State laws often establish the maximum fees that banks may charge for trust services. The cost of the staff functions needed to perform the servious may convince management that the potential income does not justify the effort. Trust departments inherently need tax, legal, investment, and analytical specialists who create higher per capita salary expenses.

Trust operations can also be characterized as both labor- and paper-intensive because of the volume of dividend checks, securities purchase-and-sale orders, coupons, and tax returns that must be processed and the detailed record-keeping that must be performed. In some cases banks have addressed this problem by "farming out" the actual data processing work to outside firms while preserving their own direct liaison with customers.

Comprehensive management information systems are also critical in fiduciary operations. The market value and composition of each individual portfolio must be known at all times, as well as the amount of each individual security held by the bank. Pro forma computer printouts may be used to show the potential effects of alternate investment management decisions. The bank's relative performance in managing equities in pension and profit-sharing plans must be measured against that of its competitors and against such yardsticks as the Dow Jones Index.

Some concern has been expressed about the outlook for trust operations. At least in part, this is attributable to reports of the declining importance of trust departments in overall bank income. During the 1960s New York City banks reported that their fiduciary areas generated some 10 percent of total operating income.[9] By contrast, 1978 statistics show that of all the major Full Service banks, Northern Trust Company (Chicago) was the only one to report that as much as 10 percent of operating income resulted from its trust services.[10]

On the other hand, there are many encouraging factors, suggesting that trust services, if properly marketed and priced, can be depended on to regain their former importance as profit-producing components. The study conducted by Louis Harris in 1972 disclosed that 3 percent of the 3168 responding consumers were already using one or more commercial bank trust services, and pointed to the increases in income and sophistication of many consumers as the rationale for predicting future growth[11] The framework of federal and state tax laws has led greater numbers of individuals to seek tax shelters and become more responsive to investment management and estate planning services. A study conducted by the United States Trust Company in 1979 showed that 520,000 Americans had a net worth of at least $1 million.[12] Such individuals are automatic candidates for personal trust services. Corporations, too, can take increased advantage of trust facilities.[13]

With commercial banks' capability to provide all types of personal, corporate, and institutional trust services well established, it would appear from this catalogue of potential opportunities that they will be able to expand their fiduciary operations in the future and derive improved earnings from this source, thus reversing the downturn experienced in recent years.

CASH MANAGEMENT SERVICES

As noted in Chapter 4, one of the most fundamental changes in American commercial banking can be attributed largely to the new thinking of those corporate financial officers and affluent individuals who control demand deposit balances. They no longer leave large quantities of ex-

[9]Crosse and Hempel, *op. cit.*, p. 10.
[10]"The 50 Largest Trust Operations," *Forbes*, April 16, 1979, p. 135.
[11]*The Second Study: The American Public's and Community Opinion Leaders' Views of Banks and Bankers in 1972*, Philadelphia, The Foundation for Full Service Banks, 1972, p. 77.
[12]*Time*, July 9, 1979, p. 54.
[13]Terrence F. Martell and Robert L. Fitts, "Potential Customers of Bank Trust Departments," *The Bankers Magazine*, May-June 1979, p. 74.

cess funds in accounts that earn no interest for them. Checking account balances are used to offset the costs of services provided by the banks; surplus funds are put to work to generate income. A wide range of investment opportunities exists today, and the holder of $1 million may find it possible to earn as much as $400 through its investment for one 24-hour period. Consequently there is an increasing willingness to listen to any suggestions a bank may be able to make for the improved and expedited handling of corporate funds. The generic term for the range of bank services that provide the improved and expedited processing is *cash management.*

One of the basic premises in the total concept of cash management is that an issued check is nothing more than a piece of paper until its payee can convert it into usable funds. Several days may be required for the check to travel through its life-cycle; it may be delayed by the mail, the payee may be slow in depositing it, and the bank of deposit may not be able to route it promptly to the drawee.

Almost 30 years ago commercial banks began offering a service known as lock box to their major corporate customers in order to reduce the time required for mail, deposit, and collection processing. Under lock box service, a bank acts as agent for its customer, operates a post office box into which all the customer's incoming payments are directed, opens the mail, examines checks for negotiability, makes the deposit, and routes the deposited checks to drawees in a manner that provides maximum availability. The user receives whatever form is required to provide a daily posting medium.

When it was first offered, lock box was felt to be applicable only to the major corporations that receive relatively limited quantities of checks each month, but whose incoming payments are for large dollar amounts.

New technology has made it possible to expand on the original concept. Lock box today is utilized not only by the large corporations that constituted the traditional market, but by utilities, insurers, and thrift institutions. Huge volumes of small payments can now be quickly and efficiently handled on equipment that reads the optically scannable data on each check or other document, and generates magnetic tape output. That tape is used by the customer to update receivables and generate reports of past-due payments.

Depository transfer checks exemplify another specialized cash management service responding to specific customer needs. They are no-signature, preprinted instruments, prepared by banks and used only to move funds from one account to another. Daily input is supplied to the corporation's concentration bank so that it can prepare one check on each regional bank account, into which incoming payments have already been deposited. The depository transfer check moves the deposited funds from many locations into a single bank account, giving the customer prompt availability at a per-item cost significantly less than that which a wire transfer system would generate.

For customers who issue a large volume of checks each month, account reconciliation and microfilm storage may be offered as cash management services. The former provides a computerized list, in check number order, of all paid and/or outstanding items; the latter, as an adjunct to account reconciliation, eliminates the burden of receiving, storing, and accessing paid checks for the user, since the bank retains a microfilm record of each paid item and provides an authenticated copy whenever requested for legal, tax, or audit purposes.

To control disbursements and use bank float to their own advantage, many corporations today employ a cash management technique designed to lengthen the time required for issued checks to be presented to the drawee bank and actually debited to an account. This technique serves to offset the use of lock box by the payees, whose objective is to reduce the same period. It requires the use of bank accounts located at strategically remote points, such as Montana and Alaska, so that issued checks will require additional time to reach the drawee. The Federal Reserve has gone on record as opposing this "remote disbursement" system because it increases "Fed float," now averaging over $3 billion per day.

Cash Management Information

The original concepts of cash management services related exclusively to deposits and disbursements. A third field has recently been added through the offering of services that are designed purely to furnish timely and complete information to customers about the status of their accounts.

Many major banks throughout the United States offer some type of terminal-oriented service, enabling the user to access the bank's computer under strict security conditions over local telephone lines. The terminal is located in the user's office or factory and serves a variety of information-gathering purposes. The customer may wish to receive a hard-copy printout that shows "book" and "available" balances and details each debit and credit posted to the account. Data may be obtained, through a single terminal, on accounts at each major bank, so that the customer obtains a comprehensive picture of each day's cash position. The terminal may also be used to initiate wire transfers of funds. Some banks offer a further enhancement that enables the customer to obtain information early in the morning and again at a later point during the business day, so that all debits and credits that were posted after the first access are identified.

Cash Management Consulting

As part of their cash management services, many banks now offer to perform comprehensive analyses of a customer's receipts and disbursements. In these cases the bank actually acts as a consultant and, based on the results of the analyses, recommends optimum points for lock boxes or disbursement accounts. At the customer's option, computer-generated reports of a variety of configurations can be supplied, with the potential costs and benefits shown for each.

Future Potential

The entire area of cash management services is one of the fastest-growing in modern commercial banking and appears to have an unlimited future. There seems to be no doubt that services which enable corporate, institutional, and government customers to expedite the inflow of funds, control disbursements, reduce clerical work, and obtain more complete and timely information will become increasingly popular. A survey conducted in 1973 of 161 corporate financial officers showed that 80 percent were using lock box, wire transfers, depository transfer checks, account reconciliation, or other specialized banking services; while they recognized an obligation to maintain demand deposits with the banks to "pay" for services rendered, they also identified an obligation to their employers to use any excess funds, over and above those compensating balances, for interest-earning purposes.[14]

Because deposits constitute the bank's basic raw material, compensating balances have usually been sought as a means of offsetting the ex-

[14]David I. Fisher, *Cash Management*, New York, The Conference Board, 1973, p. 48

penses incurred in providing a service. Recently, corporations have displayed a tendency to prefer direct fees rather than balances in compensation for services. In this way they free up balances that can be used for investment purposes and gain a tax deduction for the fees paid to the bank, since these constitute a direct business expense. If this trend continues, pressures will increase on the banks for detailed analyses of the advantages and disadvantages in each case. Fees may constitute an acceptable form of reimbursement *if* they are sufficient to cover expenses and generate profits. On the other hand, any shift from balances to fees creates the problem of further erosion of the bank's deposit base, with a resulting shrinkage in its loanable and investable funds.

As part of its overall profit center planning, a bank should be aware at all times of the income that results from marketing and implementing cash management services and of the expenses incurred in providing them. Only in this way can management determine whether the cash management function is actually having a favorable impact on the bank's overall bottom line. It is also helpful to conduct periodic surveys among existing users of cash management services in order to determine their level of satisfaction with the bank's performance. Additionally, these surveys may disclose new areas of customer needs. The bank can enhance its image very substantially by providing innovative responses to those needs, thus gaining a competitive advantage.

X

REGULATORY CONSTRAINTS

Because of the three far-reaching and dramatic developments during the 1960s—the negotiable C/D, the bank card, and the bank holding company—that decade has been characterized as one of the most significant in American banking history. Each of the three not only had an immediate impact on the banking industry, but also guaranteed that it would never again be the same.

The introduction of the negotiable C/D helped to convert banking from a demand- to a time-deposit orientation, moving banks from asset to liability management and creating new problems of interest expense. The introduction of the bank card opened up a new world of retail services and provided the key to consumer use of many EFTS applications. These two innovations began the decade; the third, the rise to prominence of the bank holding company (BHC) occurred near the end of the 10-year period but, like the other two, is important for its potential as well as its historical significance. At a time when competitors are exerting new, more numerous, and more intensive pressures on the commercial banking system, the BHC may provide the best vehicle for coping with those pressures and meeting the competitive challenge.

HISTORICAL DEVELOPMENT

The restrictive policies of many states on branch banking led commercial banks to seek some method of circumventing the regulations in order to serve more customers in their geographic area. One method of establishing a presence in more than one locality, even when state laws specifically prohibited actual branching, was through the system known as *chain banking*.

The Federal Reserve has defined chain banking as a system in which a network of separately chartered commercial banks is created, with the controlling stock interest in each bank held by a single group of individuals.[1] Interlocking directorates among the banks are commonplace. Although chain banking networks were typically established in states that did not allow branching, they went unchallenged by those states in most cases, and many of them exist today as components of other organizations.[2]

In the second half of the nineteenth century a new pattern of organization appeared in the form of the holding company, the operations of which became known as *group banking*.

In any type of business, a holding company may be formed as a corporate entity that exercises control over other companies through stock ownership. Although it was not legally defined as such by Congress until 1933,[3] the *bank* holding company was one in which one or more commercial banks appeared as part of the overall organization. A holding company that controlled banks in several cities or towns was able to circumvent state restrictions and operate in a manner tantamount to actual branching. By 1920 a large-scale trend in this direction had been identified, and in many cases the holding company that had one or more banks in its structure had become a multimillion-dollar enterprise, often diversified into such fields as investments, real estate, securities, and restaurant chains.[4] Many of the holding companies that controlled a bank during the depression achieved a higher survival rate than the independent banks.

Until 1933 group banking did not come under federal or state supervision, simply because a holding company was not considered on the same basis as a bank. From today's perspective on bank regulation, it is of interest to note that the courts which were consulted on group bank-

[1] "Chain Banking Systems," *Federal Reserve Bulletin*, April 1947, p. 463.

[2] Henry C. Rohlf, "One-Bank Holding Companies," Thesis, Stonier Graduate School of Banking, Rutgers University, 1971.

[3] Pauline B. Heller, *Handbook of Federal Bank Holding Company Law*, New York, Law Journal Press, 1976, p. xvii.

[4] Michael A. Jessee and Steven A. Seelig, *Bank Holding Companies and the Public Interest*, Lexington, MA, D. C. Heath, 1977, p. 7.

ing generally held that banks should be run by their principals with a minimum of interference by agencies of government.[5]

In 1927 the Federal Reserve identified a growing trend toward group banking,[6] and by 1929 holding companies included 8 percent of all commercial banks, controlling 19 percent of total bank loans and investments.[7]

In some cases, a holding company was formed specifically to unify and strengthen a number of banks. Northwest Bancorporation and First Bank System, both headquartered in the Twin Cities, exemplify this type of voluntary association, formed during the Depression. The former now controls eighty-five banks in seven states with total assets of $11 billion; First Bank System controls ninety-one banks and trust companies in five states, with total assets of $10.3 billion.[8] Many of the banks in both groups had enjoyed friendly correspondent relationships with one another. By being absorbed into the holding companies, the smaller institutions gained capital, liquidity, and community loyalty resulting from stronger financial backing, and they were able to weather the economic storm of the early 1930s.

The tidal wave of bank failures during the Depression prompted Congress to begin a series of investigations, designed to determine whether the speculative nonbank operations of holding companies had contributed to the financial crisis. One result of these hearings was the inclusion in the 1933 Banking Act of the first federal attempt to regulate the operations of holding companies that controlled any commercial banks.

BHC LEGISLATION

The 1933 Act required that bank holding companies divest themselves of any investment business and that they submit to regular examinations by federal agencies. It is the former provision, commonly called the Glass-Steagall Act, that remains in force today and prevents commercial

[5]George S. Eccles, "Registered Bank Holding Companies," in Herbert V. Prochnow and Herbert V. Prochnow, Jr. (Eds.), *Changing World of Banking*, New York, Harper & Row, 1974, p. 85.

[6]Board of Governors, *Annual Report*, 1927.

[7]Jessee and Seelig, *op. cit.*, p. 6.

[8]Joseph Asher, "Golden Jubilee for 2 Holding Companies in Twin Cities," *ABA Banking Journal*, June 1979, p. 104.

banks from underwriting revenue bonds of municipalities or becoming involved in the securities business.

In actuality the 1933 Act did little to restrict the operations of bank holding companies other than to impose the Glass-Steagall limitation. The Act did not require BHCs to register with the Federal Reserve if their group banking systems consisted exclusively of state-chartered banks; it permitted continued acquisitions of banks by each existing BHC; and it made no mention of the possible competitive effects of further expansion.[9]

Between 1933 and 1956, numerous bills were introduced in Congress to establish restrictions on BHCs; however, despite the efforts of the Comptroller of the Currency and the Fed, none was passed. The Federal Reserve expressed concern over the trend:

> Bank holding companies are being used to defeat the expressed will of Congress regarding the establishment of branches, and to gather under one management many different and varied enterprises wholly unallied and wholly unrelated to the conduct of a banking business.[10]

Congressional hearings in 1955 and 1956 finally resulted in the first federal legislation specifically aimed at the group banking movement. The Bank Holding Company Act of 1956 defined a BHC as any entity that directly or indirectly controlled 25 percent or more of the voting stock of *two or more* banks, or controlled in any way the election of a majority of the directors of *two or more* banks.[11] It also required all such BHCs to register with the Federal Reserve and ordered them to divest themselves of any component engaged in activities that were "not related to banking *per se*."[12]

Perhaps the most important feature of the 1956 Act, seen from today's perspective, was the blanket exemption granted to BHCs if they controlled only one bank. Although all the implications of that exemption were not apparent at the time, they eventually provided the basis for the creation of specific one-bank holding companies—a development that

[9] Rohlf, *op. cit.*, pp. 10-11.
[10] Board of Governors, *Annual Report, 1943.*
[11] Jessee and Seelig, *op. cit.*, p. 10.
[12] Heller, *op. cit.*, p. 21.

John Bunting, former Chairman of First Pennsylvania Corporation, has called "one of banking's few authentic revolutions."[13]

During the 1960s commercial banks found themselves hampered in their efforts to grow and diversify, limited in their ability to improve profits, and subjected to greater competitive pressures than ever before. The introduction of the negotiable Certificate of Deposit had made them liability managers and created problems of interest expense. Competitors, especially savings and loan associations, were steadily attracting deposits at the expense of commercial banks. Institutions that were members of multibank BHCs were restricted in their efforts to enter other businesses by the 1956 Act; those that were not members of holding companies found themselves defendants in litigation brought by data processing, travel, insurance, or other firms anxious to prevent them from competing.[14]

In attempting to cope with these pressures, banks resorted to a variety of management techniques. One was to increase investment in municipals, thus improving income through the federal tax exemption on earnings. Another was to expand traditional loan-to-deposit ratios, with a corresponding increase in both interest income and risk. A third was to implement cost-cutting programs, although the inflation rate of the 1960s hampered this effort.[15]

The most attractive alternative, however, was to diversify into various financial services and activities. In this respect, national banks were allowed more freedom than their state-chartered counterparts through a series of rulings by James Smith, then Comptroller of the Currency. It was his position that national banks could perform financial services that were "closely related to banking" as long as their solvency and liquidity, in his judgment, were not being impaired. His rulings precipitated a number of requests by state-chartered banks for conversion to national charters and a subsequent relaxation in the policies of regulatory agencies. The Fed similarly responded by amending Regulation Y, which governs group banking, thus giving a more liberal interpretation to the concept of nonbank interests and services.[16]

[13]"One-Bank Holding Companies: A Banker's View," *Harvard Business Review*, May-June 1969, p. 99.

[14]Paul S. Nadler, "The One-Bank Holding Company," in Prochnow and Prochnow, *op. cit.*, p. 144.

[15]Edward W. Reed, Richard V. Cotter, Edward K. Gill, and Richard K. Smith, *Commercial Banking*, Englewood Cliffs, NJ, Prentice-Hall, 1976, p. 48.

[16]Jessee and Seelig, *op. cit.*, p. 33.

It remained obvious, however, that maximum freedom to diversify would require a different form of organism. The realization gradually dawned that the 1956 Act applied only to BHCs that controlled two or more banks; hence banks could engage in factoring, leasing, mortgage financing, real estate investment, and insurance by availing themselves of that exemption.

The situation was brought to a head in 1965 when the Meadow Brook National Bank, a major New York institution that subsequently became National Bank of North America, [17] was acquired by the CIT Financial Corporation. This acquisition was widely resented by commercial banks because it was legal for a nonbank corporation to buy a bank, whereas the converse was legally prohibited or restricted.

The then First National City Bank of New York was the first major commercial bank to counter the CIT action. It established a new holding company, Citicorp, with the bank as the most important component. The significant point was that only one bank was involved; hence the 1956 Act did not restrict the actions of the new holding company. Citicorp then began to diversify into various areas of financially related business that multibank holding companies could not legally enter.[18] In steadily increasing numbers, other banks followed this pattern, exchanging all the outstanding shares of stock in a single bank for shares in a new corporation. The latter then formed subsidiaries to perform various services.

As bank after bank hastened to join the movement, fears and reservations about the ultimate effects were expressed in many quarters. William McChesney Martin, then Chairman of the Federal Reserve Board of Governors, served as spokesman for many concerned individuals:

> The greatest risk is in concentration of economic power. . . . A bank might deny credit to competing firms or grant credit to other borrowers only on condition that they agree to do business with the affiliated firm.[19]

Questions were also raised regarding the posture a one-bank BHC would assume if one of its affiliates were experiencing financial difficulties. Would the bank's resources then be used, perhaps at the expense of

[17]This is the same institution that was acquired by National Westminster Bank in 1979.
[18]Martin Mayer, *The Bankers*, New York, David McKay Co., 1974, pp. 384-385.
[19]Federal Reserve Bank of Chicago, *Conference on Bank Structure and Competition*, April 1977, p. 117.

depositors' interests, to help the affiliate survive? Another Federal Reserve Governor, Andrew Brimmer, stated the case emphatically:

> Banks have got a mother-hen complex. Every bank holding company will do whatever it can, at considerable cost, to avoid failure of an affiliate.[20]

In some cases banks themselves must be held responsible for the concern originally expressed by Brimmer and frequently restated by others.[21] First Wisconsin Corporation, parent of the First Wisconsin National Bank, bought $14.8 million in loans from its REIT, admitting the possibility of incurring losses as a result but claiming that the action was necessary to protect the BHC's stockholders.[22] United California Bank took similar action when a foreign subsidiary failed.[23]

While the banks, individually and through policy statements of the American Bankers Association, expressed their intention of operating prudently and confining their activities to areas directly related to banking itself, the concerns and fears of their critics continued to be heard. The trend toward assumption of even more economic power by major banks was a prime topic.[24]

Chairman Wright Patman of the House Committee on Banking and Currency led a movement to revise the Act of 1956, and largely through his efforts a series of amendments to it became the content of Public Law 91-607, signed into law by President Richard Nixon on December 31, 1970 and subsequently incorporated by the Fed into Regulation Y. These amendments served two basic purposes:

1. They brought *all* BHCs, specifically those that involved only one bank, under the jurisdiction of the Federal Reserve and gave the Fed full power to determine which activities were permitted.
2. Through a "grandfather clause" they allowed BHCs, with specific Fed approval, to continue to engage in nonbank activities that

[20] In "An Early Warning System to Spot Sick Banks," *Business Week*, October 26, 1974, p. 92.

[21] Jack M. Guttenberg and Bernard Shull, "Bank Holding Companies and Abuse of the Power to Grant Credit," in *Conference on Bank Structure*, p. 129.

[22] *Business Week*, October 26, 1974, p. 92

[23] Martin Mayer, *The Bankers*, p. 389

[24] "The New Breed in Banking," *Business Week*, September 15, 1973, p. 90.

would otherwise be prohibited, provided the activities had been engaged in continously since June 30, 1968.[25]

Section 4(c) (8) of the amendments gave the Fed the right to determine if any nonbank activity proposed by a BHC was "so closely related to banking, or managing or controlling banks, as to be a proper incident thereto."[26] The same Section required that the Fed be the judge of whether performing that activity would produce public benefits outweighing any possible adverse affects.[27]

Within one month after the amendments had been signed into law, the Federal Reserve published its first list of approved and prohibited activities for BHCs. Since that initial list was published, the Fed has rendered many decisions on BHC applications to acquire companies or offer new services. The approved list has been expanded from time to time, and Section 225.4 of Regulation Y now states that a BHC, having filed an application to engage in any permitted activity, may automatically begin doing so unless the Fed renders an adverse ruling within 45 days.[28] The most recent listing include nineteen approved and ten prohibited services and activities (Table 10-1).

Some acquisitions by BHCs of finance companies in other states have been approved; others have been denied on the grounds that the benefits did not outweigh the possible adverse effects. In one noteworthy case the application of a major one-bank BHC for acquisition of a nuclear fuel leasing corporation was denied. It was the feeling of the Federal Reserve that the bank would have been required to supply heavy financing, and might have "sapped its financial strength" in so doing.[29]

"Tie-in" transactions, in which a customer who purchases one service from a bank is required to purchase another, are prohibited under the 1970 Act, as are all restrictions imposed by banks on customers' dealings with other banks. The net effect is to preclude any actions that might be construed as restraint of trade.[30]

Since 1970 the growth of BHCs has been truly phenomenal. By year-end 1974 a total of 1752 BHCs had registered with the Fed. These

[25]Jessee and Seelig, *op.cit.*, p. 20.
[26]Reed et al., *op. cit.*, p. 50.
[27]Jessee and Seelig, *op. cit.*, p. 20.
[28]*Federal Reserve Bulletin*, January 1979, p. 64.
[29]73 FRB 698, in Jessee and Seelig, *op. cit.*, p. 71.
[30]Reed et al., *op. cit.*, p. 51.

Table 10-1 Summary of Section 4 (C) (8) activities permitted and prohibited, July 31, 1979

Activities permitted as "closely related to banking"
- Making loans for own account or account of others
- Operating as an industrial bank or industrial loan company
- Servicing loans
- Conducting fiduciary activities
- Acting as investment or financial adviser under specified conditions
- Leasing personal and real property with full payout
- Making equity or debt investments in corporations to promote community welfare
- Providing bookkeeping or data processing services
- Operating insurance agencies
- Underwriting credit life, accident, and health insurance directly related to credit extensions by the BHC
- Engaging in the traveler's check business
- Trading and arbitraging gold and silver bullion
- Operating courier services
- Providing management consulting services to nonaffiliated banks
- Issuing money orders and general purpose variable denominated payment instruments
- Acting as futures commission merchant to execute futures contracts covering gold and silver bullion and coins
- Underwriting certain federal, state, and municipal securities
- Selling, at retail, money orders and similar instruments
- Check verification activities

Activities prohibited as "not closely related to banking"
- Insurance premium funding, i.e., the combined sale of mutual funds and insurance
- Underwriting life insurance not sold in connection with a credit transaction by a BHC or subsidiary thereof
- Real estate brokerage
- Land development
- Real estate syndication
- Management consulting
- Property management services
- Underwriting mortgage guarantee insurance "at this time"
- Operation of a travel agency
- Operation of a savings and loan association

Source. Gerald C. Fischer, "The Structure of the Commercial Banking System, 1960-1985," *Journal of Commercial Bank Lending*, September 1979, p. 60.

represented 3462 banks with deposits of $510 billion, or 68.1 percent of total commercial bank deposits at that time.[31] More recent figures show that the ten largest commercial banks are all members of holding companies and alone have deposits of $350 billion. The 100 largest BHCs at year-end 1978 held deposits of over $682 billion.[32] As a group, all BHCs now control 53.2 percent of all banking offices and 75 percent of all deposits.[33]

INTERSTATE BANKING

One provision of the original 1956 Act allowed a bank holding company in one state to acquire a bank in another if the legislatures of both states consented. To date no such action has occurred, although several states— particularly New York—have expressed their willingness to enter into this type of reciprocal plan.

New York's then Superintendent of Banks, Harry Albright, proposed in 1973 that banks in such key money centers as Los Angeles, Boston, San Francisco, Chicago, and Houston be allowed to open full-scale branches in New York City if banks from the New York were permitted to do the same.[34] His successor, John Heimann (subsequently Comptroller of the Currency) proposed similar legislation to both houses of the New York legislature in 1976.[35] More recently, William Isaac, in his first speech as a member of the FDIC Board of Governors, urged consideration for the phasing out of restrictions on interstate branch banking, provided that small, independent banks were fully protected.[36]

The 1970 Act extended "grandfather" protection to existing interstate BHCs and reinforced the McFadden Act of 1927, maintaining that state laws were paramount in all questions of branching. The most recent amendment to Regulation Y reaffirms the jurisdictional rights of the states as superior to any provisions of the BHC Act.[37]

With full-scale interstate branching still not legally possible, BHCs

[31] Heller, *op. cit.*, p. xix.

[32] "100 Largest Bank Holding Companies: A Statistical Profile," *Forbes*, April 16, 1979, pp. 136–137.

[33] Gerald C. Fischer, "The Structure of the Commercial Banking System," *Journal of Commercial Bank Lending*, September 1979, p. 58.

[34] Address to the New York State Bankers Association, Lake Placid, NY, June 14, 1973.

[35] New York Assembly 12522 and New York Senate 10074, 1976.

[36] Address to the Wisconsin Bankers Association, Milwaukee, WI, July 20, 1978.

[37] 12 CFR 225, Section 7.

have concentrated instead on expansion in many areas of nonbank services, which the McFadden Act does not cover. Through acquisitions and *de novo* installations, they have established leasing, factoring, data processing, consumer finance, and mortgage financing and servicing offices in many parts of the United States and, with specific Fed approval, have acquired savings and loan associations in key locations.[38] Obviously, at least some of these could be converted into actual branches if enabling legislation were ever passed.

The anomalies of America's patchwork quilt of bank regulation are nowhere more apparent than in the area of state regulation of branch banking. As of July 1979 twenty-two states allow unlimited branching within their borders, sixteen permit it within certain specified limits, and twelve prohibit it. Of the "limited branching" states, eleven permit multibank holding companies and five do not. Similarly, the "unit banking" states are divided; seven allow multibank BHCs while five prohibit them. Illinois, Kansas, Nebraska, Oklahoma, and West Virginia constitute the last group, thus maintaining to the utmost the basic concept of individual, single-office banks.[39] Thus although one of the original goals of group banking may have been circumvention of state laws on branching, there remain many areas where it still cannot fully attain that objective.

Nevertheless, the holding company continues to represent the single best hope of banking for the future if growth and profitability are to occur. It is only through this vehicle that a full range of financially oriented services can be provided, so that commercial banks can compete fully with such entities as credit unions, retailers, and savings and loan associations.

The point must be stressed that the implementation of BHC functions has been beneficial to customers as well as to the banks themselves. The record of the Fed in considering requests for acquisition of nonbank entities by BHCs clearly indicates that approval was granted only after clear benefits to the public sector could be identified. In a study of twenty-four such approvals, such advantages as lower interest rates on loans, lower service charges, choices for sources of a particular service, and continuation of services in a geographic area were cited by the Fed as justifying factors.[40]

[38] Jessee and Seelig, *op. cit.*, p. 141.
[39] Fischer, *op. cit.*, p. 55.
[40] Jessee and Seelig, *op. cit.*, p. 64.

Fears that expansion of BHCs would create undue concentrations of economic power do not appear to have been justified. One study showed that the percentage of statewide deposits held by BHC member banks grew by 10 percent or more in only six states from 1968 to 1973; in twenty-two cases the percentage actually declined, leading to the conclusion that small, independent banks were perfectly capable of maintaining their market shares.[41] Nonbank service organizations have also demonstrated benefits that outweigh any reduction of elimination of competition.[42]

The shrinkage of excess demand deposits in the banking system has not caused a corresponding decline in the demand for financial services; quite the contrary. The corporate financial officer who has found it both feasible and profitable to draw down surplus balances and invest them also seeks that "package" of services which will permit still further improvement in overall cash management. For major corporations today, balances are concentrated in those banks that prove most responsive to total financial needs. Loans, lines of credit, leasing and factoring, international, trust, concentration, and disbursement services provide the justification for keeping balances with banks; those institutions that cannot or do not provide these services are most likely to suffer competitively. To meet their corporate customers' needs, it is logical for them to establish subsidiaries through the holding company to provide a coordinated group of products. For identical reasons, the successful banks in the consumer market are those that provide the full range of loans, automated facilities, bank cards, and other services tailored to personal needs. The BHC framework offers the best possibility for meeting both wholesale and retail banking needs and serving as wide a clientele as possible, both at home and abroad.

BANK MERGERS AND BRANCHING

The 1950s witnessed many of the largest mergers in U.S. banking history, particularly in the New York City area. At year-end 1978 six of the ten largest banks in the country, each of them a component in a BHC, were headquartered in New York City. Each of them had partici-

[41] *Ibid.*, pp. 142-143.
[42] *Ibid.*

pated in a merger during that decade. The need or desire to expand a specialized service area or to acquire branches and thus enter the retail field was often the rationale for the merger.

From the legislative standpoint there was little in the way of formal statutes to limit such mergers. The one standard that appears to have been the primary consideration in each case was the degree of capital adequacy.[43] However, as the trend continued, questions were raised as to the competitive effects of mergers and the resulting concentration of power. In 1960 Congress addressed these questions and drew up the Bank Merger Act, whose principal provision stated that a single authority would henceforth rule on all acquisitions and mergers involving commercial banks. The decision of that authority would be final in all cases. For all national banks, the Comptroller of the Currency would have jurisdiction; for state member banks, the Fed; for insured state nonmembers, the FDIC; and for all others, the individual state banking departments. It was the stated intention of the Senate Banking and Currency Commettee to have this Act eliminate all jurisdictional questions and conflicts among the several authorities.[44]

The 1960 Act ordered that the single designated authority consider four factors in each application for merger: the history and financial condition of each bank, the competency and character of the management teams, the prospects of the merged bank for profitability and growth, and the interests of the community to be served. Mergers were not to be approved unless the probable benefits to depositors and the community clearly offset any adverse effects of competition.[45]

The U.S. Supreme Court then brought commercial banking under the provisions of the Clayton and Sherman Antitrust Acts through its decisions in the Philadelphia and Lexington cases.[46] In doing so, the Court not only subjected banking to antitrust laws for the first time; it also contravened the will of Congress as expressed in the 1960 Act. The two decisions made antitrust considerations the ultimate test to be applied to bank acquisitions and mergers, rather than the ruling of a designated authority. This enabled the Office of the Attorney General

[43] Howard D. Crosse and George H. Hempel, *Management Policies for Commercial Banks*, 2nd ed., Englewood Cliffs, NJ, 1973, p. 27.

[44] *Ibid.*, p. 29.

[45] "Federal Laws Regulating Bank Mergers," Federal Reserve Bank of Cleveland, *Economic Review*, January 1971, p. 18.

[46] Details of both decisions may be found in Crosse and Hempel, *op. cit.*, p. 30.

to intervene in mergers whenever such action seemed appropriate. The Justice Department, in effect, was empowered to determine the potential anticompetitive effects of a merger and to oppose it in a federal court.

However, the question was left unanswered as to whether previously approved mergers were now to be subject to challenge by the Justice Department, with possible legal reversal. The 1966 modification of the 1960 Act contained a "grandfather clause," protecting some 2200 such mergers. This modification also created a mandatory 30-day waiting period following approval of a merger by the designated authority. During that period the Justice Department could initiate action if it so desired.

In two subsequent decisions, the Supreme Court made it clear that the burden of proof in all merger or acquisition proposals is on the banks themselves, rather than on the Justice Department. The banks must be prepared to show that the benefits of the proposal outweigh the reduction in competition and that those benefits cannot reasonably be attained through other means. The Court did not identify the specific market share percentages that would constitute evidence of a significant reduction in competition.[47]

As a result of the Supreme Court's rulings, banks have displayed increased reluctance to enter into merger negotiations. They are well aware that some mergers, approved by designated authorities but opposed by the Justice Department, were in litigation for years. It is pointless to begin negotiations for a merger or an acquisition as long as ambiguity and doubt exist about the factors that will enter into an ultimate legal decision.

BRANCH BANKING

The controversial topic of branching is frequently mentioned throughout this text. Branch banking is one of the most visible components in a banking pattern of diversity, greater than that existing in any other banking system in the world. There is diversity among types of banks (wholesale and retail, unit and branch, member and nonmember) and among the regulatory agencies that supervise them. This diversity is the

[47]Crosse and Hempel, *op. cit.*, pp. 30–31.

result of the long-standing, frequently reinforced view that banking in America should be decentralized and that each state should be the ultimate authority within its borders. Federal statutes and Supreme Court decisions have repeatedly upheld the rights of each state to regulate branch banking; hence the three different conditions previously cited: twenty-two states allow statewide branching, sixteen permit limited branching, and twelve do not allow branching at all. It is reasonable to assume that, without such statutes and decisions, American banking might have developed along the same lines as the systems found in other nations, with a strong central bank (frequently a direct instrumentality of the government) operating jointly with a few large institutions.

Fears of this type of concentration of power characterized much of the early history of American banking. New York, Massachusetts, and Rhode Island, for example, all had laws on their books at one time, stating that no one could operate a banking business except at his own legal place of residence.[48] The abuses of the "wildcat banking" era, when banks opened remote, nearly inaccessible facilities for the presentation and redemption of their notes, were cited as evidence that branch banking was inherently wrong. As recently as 1925, only 3.1 percent of state banks and 1.3 percent of national banks operated branches.[49]

In those states that persist as "unit banking" jurisdictions, where no branching is allowed, various associations of small, independent banks continue to offer the view that unlimited branching inevitably leads to excessive concentration of power in the hands of a few institutions. They believe that the one-office neighborhood bank, operated by local management, serves customers at least as well as any larger entity could.

The McFadden Act, which extends branching options to national banks in their individual states *only* to the extent that state-chartered banks have the same options (and thus makes national banks subject to state laws, rather than to the Comptroller of the Currency), is the legislation most frequently cited in contemporary discussions of branching. President A. W. Clausen of Bank of America has described it as a "very costly legislative antique"[50] at a time when American commercial banks cannot buy institutions in other states but foreign banks can; when other

[48]Crosse and Hempel, *op. cit.*, p. 17.
[49]Peter J. Brennan, "The McFadden Act," *ABA Banking Journal*, September 1979, p. 49.
[50]In Brennan, *op. cit.*, p. 49.

financial institutions can operate without any similar form of constraint; when retailers can offer financial services (e.g., Sears Roebuck) in every part of the country; and when EFT services and 24-hour foreign exchange markets make such restrictive laws anachronisms. The incumbent Comptroller of the Currency believes that statutory restrictions on branch banking present an urgent problem in that they impose a burden on communities and citizens.[51] Both the Presidential Commission on Money and Credit and the Comptroller of the Currency's Advisory Committee have recommended that banks be allowed to branch within trading areas, and the President's Commission on Financial Structure and Regulation (the "Hunt Commission") has expressed the view that less-restricted branching might well be in the public interest.[52] This entire topic will necessarily have to receive still more attention in the future.

FEDERAL REGULATION OF BANKING

Without exception every commercial bank in the United States is subject to one or more regulatory units of governments. Through the chartering process a set of government controls is imposed before a bank can open its doors and accept deposits. Throughout a bank's entire life-cycle, representatives of government examine it, scrutinize its financial reports, and make decisions about its ability to expand and offer services.

The early colonists believed that a minimum of government regulation of banking was desirable. Their basic premise was that banks should be given the same freedom to operate as other merchants. That notion vanished in the nineteenth century, by which time it had become apparent that banking is, per se, different from all other industries. Bankers must accept the notion that what they do, and the manner in which they do it, must be viewed as legitimate areas for concern and supervision by governments. An industry that handles a trillion dollars of deposited funds, and whose daily operations so vitally affect the entire economy, cannot expect to escape regulation.

The difficulty lies in the extent of this regulation and in its overlap-

[51]John Heimann, in "Banking in Transition," *The Bankers Magazine*, September-October 1978, p. 22.
[52]Reed et al., *op. cit.*, p. 42.

ping nature in so many cases. National banks, for example, are under the jurisdiction of the Comptroller of the Currency, yet by law must be members of the Federal Reserve and FDIC. The Comptroller is responsible for the annual audit of each such institution, but the other two federal agencies may conduct their own examinations whenever they feel it is necessary or appropriate. All state-chartered member banks are regularly examined by the Federal Reserve, but are also subject to examination and regulation by the FDIC, to which they must belong. State banking authorities also examine and regulate this category of banks. A state-chartered, insured nonmember is similarly subject to both the FDIC and the regulations of its own state. Only 2 percent of all commercial banks in the United States fall into the final category; they are uninsured nonmembers, subject only to state laws and examinations.

In addition to regulating state-chartered members, the Federal Reserve is also responsible for all BHCs, the foreign branches of member banks, and Edge Act subsidiaries of all banks. Mergers are subject to the approval of the Justice Department.

The National Banking and Currency Acts of 1863 and 1864 created a dual banking system, under which a bank may have either a national or state charter. Today it is interesting to note that two prominent figures on the banking scene have used an identical phrase, "competition in laxity," to describe this system. During his term as Chairman of the Federal Reserve Board of Governors, Dr. Arthur Burns stated that the regulatory system "fosters competition in laxity . . . [and] should be substantially reorganized."[53] Senator William Proxmire, Chairman of the Senate Committee on Banking, Housing, and Urban Affairs, made this comment 4 years later:

> Banks are free to pick and choose which of the three federal agencies shall regulate them. This system leads to competition in laxity with regulation at the lowest common denominator level.[54]

Their choice of words reflects the view that a federal agency might lower its standards to attract or maintain its membership.[55] Proxmire has gone on record in favor of consolidation of the office of the Comptroller of the Currency, the Fed, and the FDIC into a single unit to

[53] "An Early Warning System to Spot Sick Banks," *Business Week*, October 26, 1974, p. 88.
[54] In "Banking in Transition," p. 29.
[55] Reed et al., *op. cit.*, p. 14.

prevent this possibility and to eliminate what he has called "burdensome and overlapping duplication."[56] However, his proposal has been criticized by the Comptroller on the grounds that it grants too much power to one organization and puts an end to state regulation of banking.[57] State bank associations and supervisors have also expressed their opposition to the Proxmire proposal, since they view it as inimical to the continued existence of the dual banking system.[58]

Critics of the existing regulatory structure claim that it does not treat state and national banks on the same basis, generates pressures for the lowering of standards by the agencies involved, causes duplication of effort with accompanying inefficiency and expense, and creates delays in the initiation of action to curb unsound practices. Those who favor continuation of the existing system claim that it works well, prevents undue concentration of power in a single authority, and provides for flexibility in regulation.[59]

It has also been pointed out that under the present system the Federal Reserve, by virtue of its role as the supervisor of all bank holding companies, has assumed a role significantly superior to that of the other agencies and may be able to circumvent their rights and powers. The same critics feel that the rapid expansion of the holding company movement has occupied so much of the Federal Reserve's time and effort that attention to monetary policy may have been neglected. The 1970 Act places the Fed in a position of authority over nonmember banks, as well as members, in BHCs; in the opinion of some observers this degree of control may not be entirely appropriate.[60]

For its own part, the Federal Reserve must be concerned about its diminished authority, resulting from so many banks withdrawing from the system. There has been a significant trend in this direction in recent years.

Former Chairman Frank Wille of the FDIC has suggested an approach that would entail formation of two new agencies, each headed by a federal official. One would oversee all state banks and assume the

[56]In "Banking In Transition," p. 29.

[57]Walter E. Headley, "Moderate Growth Will Help Face Seven Crucial Decisions," *American Banker*, February 2, 1977, p. 7.

[58]Lucille S. Mayne, "Restructuring the Federal Bank Regulatory System," *The Bankers Magazine*, September-October 1978, p. 72.

[59]Jessee and Seelig, *op. cit.*, p. 157.

[60]Jessee and Seelig, *op. cit.*, p. 157.

regulatory powers that the Fed now holds over state-chartered members. A counterpart unit would be responsible for all national banks. Holding companies would be supervised and examined by either, depending on the type of charter held by the lead bank. The Wille proposal also calls for a five-member Federal Banking Board. The heads of the two agencies would serve on it with one Governor from the Federal Reserve Board and two individuals named by the President. The function of this agency would be to set uniform policy for all commercial banks.[61]

The Supreme Court decision in the Philadelphia case[62] created a new problem in the overal pattern of bank regulation and supervision in that it held that banking was a unique line of commerce and that commercial banks compete *only* with other commercial banks. Hence the Court took the position that any merger might per se constitute restraint of competition, since the number of competing banks would automatically be reduced.[63]

This logic, which many bankers found difficult to understand in 1963, is even more unfathomable in today's environment. Commercial banks do not compete only with one another; they compete with an almost infinite range of organizations that seek to attract funds and offer financial services.[64]

Thrift institutions offer time and, more recently, demand deposit accounts and extend home mortgage and improvement loans, together with overdraft privileges on checking accounts. Factoring, commercial credit, and insurance companies extend various types of loans; department stores and personal finance companies extend huge amounts of credit to consumers; and credit unions have become a major force in the deposit, payment, and credit areas that were traditionally confined to commercial banks. Major corporations—themselves the banks' largest customers—lend to each other through commercial paper, bypassing the banking system completely. The number of nonbank credit card issuers continues to increase. Recently, several money-market funds have begun aggressively seeking the deposits of individuals, thus prompting one columnist to point out that the need for any kind of bank account is diminishing each year.[65]

[61] Jessee and Seelig, *op. cit.*, p. 157

[62] Mayne, *op. cit.*, p. 74

[63] U.S. vs. Philadelphia National Bank, 374 U.S. 321.

[64] Paul S. Nadler, *Commercial Banking in the Economy*, 2nd ed., New York, Random House, 1973, p. 176.

[65] Jane B. Quinn, "Savings Without Banks," *Newsweek*, July 16, 1979, p. 82.

The federal banking legislation that was passed 50 years ago, and is still largely intact, had an essentially negative tenor; it reflected the view that bankers had been guilty of excessive competition with one another and had neglected the proper business of banking. Therefore the areas of activity open to the commercial banks became limited. This may have curbed previous excesses, but it left little room for any type of innovation or flexibility. The holding company has been an effective countering device; indeed with both the Supreme Court and Justice Department apparently assuming a posture of automatic opposition to acquisition and merger proposals,[66] it is perceived as the only vehicle through which banks can broaden their range of services and thus compete effectively for funds. Yet the BHC still raises regulatory problems when its component is a national bank; the holding company itself automatically comes under the supervision of the Federal Reserve, but the bank that is its major entity remains under the Comptroller of the Currency.

The nation's largest commercial bank, Bank of America National Trust and Savings Association, may be cited as an example. Its parent, Bankamerica Corporation, listed a total of twenty-three domestic banking subsidiaries (including Edge Act corporations in four states), five foreign banking subsidiaries, and thirteen nonbank subsidiaries as evidence of its ability to serve customers through computer processing, real estate, insurance, and other financially related functions throughout the world.[67] The Comptroller of the Currency is the bank's primary regulator; the Federal Reserve is responsible for overseeing the operation of the holding company; and various state laws may affect particular operations of the BHC that fall within state jurisdictions. If the Fed, as the agency responsible for the holding company, is to conduct an examination of its total financial position, it must rely on the Comptroller's audit of the bank and conduct its own check of the operations of all the nonbank affiliates and subsidiaries.

In their efforts to compete more effectively within the framework of so much regulation and federal and state supervision and control, commercial banks have recently begun to take advantage of the Federal Reserve's list of permissible BHC activities and have acquired or are seeking to acquire a type of financial institution known as the industrial bank. Technically these are not banks or savings and loan associations at

[66]Nadler, *Commercial Banking in the Economy*, pp. 177-178.
[67]*Annual Report*, 1976.

all, but are state-chartered organizations, legal in eleven states, that are authorized to render a limited range of financial services. Industrial banks can accept consumer deposits and extend various forms of business and personal credit. Citicorp, Manufacturers Hanover Corporation, Bankamerica Corporation, Chemical New York Corporation, and First Pennsylvania Corporation are among the major BHCs that have obtained approval from the Fed to acquire existing industrial banks or to establish *de novo* institutions of this type. Since the Regulation Q interest-rate ceilings do not apply to industrial banks, they can compete more effectively with thrift institutions.[68]

At first glance it may appear that the banks have little reason to complain; the earnings records of the major bank holding companies in recent years might suggest that BHCs do not need remedial legislation and that they are able to function very profitably despite their claims of excessive and archaic regulation. This superficial analysis, however, ignores two significant points. In the second quarter of 1979, only three of the ten largest BHCs were able to increase their rate of return on equity by more than the national inflation rate of 13 percent, and all ten of them are highly leveraged institutions whose borrowed funds, including deposits, are twenty-one to twenty-eight times as large as their invested equities.[69]

Walter Wriston has provided one of the most succinct yet meaningful statements of his banks' general viewpoint:

> The solution is *not* to take away the freedoms that make our non-banking competition more vigorous. It is to let us compete under regulations framed . . . on the real world . . . [and] to give us the flexibility to provide that competition which always improves services to the public.[70]

A final summation of the same position has been provided by Kenneth A. Randall, former Chairman of the FDIC and more recently President of United Virginia Bankshares, Inc.:

> In our imperfect world, there is the branch that we may want to start but that the branching laws will not permit, the banking market that we can't

[68]Karen W. Arenson, "A Bank Bridge over State Lines," *The New York Times*, April 20, 1979, p. D-1.

[69]Robert A. Bennett, "Inflation Makes Inroads at Big Banks," *The New York Times*, July 23, 1979, p. D-1.

[70]In "Banking in Transition," p. 35.

> reach because it's just into the next state or county, . . . [and] the financial service that has not been approved by the Federal Reserve.[71]

Accepting deposits was once considered a unique banking franchise, and therefore all types of federal and state restrictions were considered justified for the commercial banking system. The justification has long since disappeared, but the restrictions remain.

[71] In Herbert V. Prochnow Jr., and Herbert V. Prochnow, (Eds.), *The Changing World of Banking*, New York, Harper & Row, 1974, p. 324.

XI

THE NEW WORLD OF BANKING

The commercial banker used to be primarily an asset manager, who loaned and invested, on a highly selective basis, the demand deposits that flowed steadily into the system. Acronyms such as MICR, NOW, BCH, and EFTS had not yet been invented. Networks of overseas branch facilities did not exist; international transactions were handled largely through foreign correspondent banks. Only one major commercial bank in New York City actively encouraged installment loan applications from individual wage-earners (and captured over 50 percent of the market as a result); its competitors expressed little or no interest in that type of credit facility and focused their attention solely on commercial lending. Checking account statements were sent out to all customers on the last business day of every month. Individuals who requested savings accounts or home mortgage loans were politely referred to correspondent thrift institutions, except when so-called compound interest or thrift accounts were opened as a special accomodation to existing checking account customers. All checks that would create overdrafts in accounts were individually referred to account officers for approval before being posted. Automated teller facilities and demand deposit accounting systems did not exist. The vocabulary of commercial banking did not include credit cards, C/Ds, share drafts, or Eurodollars.

Does the foregoing paragraph describe the state of the art in some ancient, long-forgotten period in American banking history? Not at all.

Every condition, management philosophy, and service (or lack of service) mentioned in it existed in 1950, when the author of this text began his career with one of the country's largest commercial banks. The changes that have occurred in every instance give some inkling of the revolution that has occurred in banking in the intervening years.

The word "revolution" is by no means an overstatement in this case. It is the only term that reflects the massive and permanent changes during those three decades. Martin Mayer's comment is of interest:

> Like all revolutions, the one in banking can be admired or loathed, depending on one's other attitudes. What it should not be is ignored—yet not one American in a thousand has any idea what has happened.[1]

All available evidence contradicts Mayer's statement in every aspect. The average American is fully aware that a revolution has indeed taken place. The banking industry, whose leaders have been described as unable to adjust to changing times and lacking in vision,[2] has been completely transformed in a multitude of ways, and the consumer has been quick to take advantage of this.

Every holder of a bank card or certificate of deposit, every depositor with a NOW account, every person who uses an automated teller facility or point-of-sale terminal, every corporate financial officer who utilizes the tremendously expanded range of banking services now available, and every individual who is exposed to radio, newspaper, magazine, billboard, and television advertising cannot help but be aware of the new world of banking.

In this text, the dynamics of change have been repeatedly stressed. The shift from asset allocation to liability management, the advent of financial conglomerates under the holding company umbrella, the dawning of a "less-check" society, and the expansion of global facilities by both American and foreign banks have been mentioned. They offer further evidence that the revolution not only has taken place, but *is* noticed.

The new world of banking is one in which the profession, once char-

[1] *The Bankers*, New York, David McKay Co., 1974, p. 5. Reprinted by permission.

[2] K. A. Randall, "An Analysis of Specific Weaknesses in Bank Management," in Herbert V. Prochnow and Herbert V. Prochnow, Jr. (Eds.), *The Changing World of Banking*, New York, Harper & Row, 1974, p. 322.

acterized by Nadler as one whose motto was "never do something the first time,"[3] now recognizes that traditional attitudes, stereotyped approaches, and hidebound thinking are no longer viable. The "old breed" of banker looked on his profession as one that could rely on a regular inflow of interest-free demand deposits and dealt selectively with a limited wholesale market. Advertising was an unnecessary evil; the entire commercial banking industry spent less than $50 million on it in 1950.[4] If, as Mayer has stated, most Americans are unaware of the changes that have taken place, the tremendous increase in advertising expenses since 1950 has been wasted.

That advertising effort is in itself evidence of banking's new attitudes. Traditionally the industry paid little attention to the essentials of marketing, and the very word "salesman" was considered to have a perjorative connotation. The banker was a prestigious figure in the community; the salesman was a door-to-door peddler or a used-car dealer.

To the contemporary banker marketing is the key to success, and the bank's Marketing Department is an integrated unit that not only supplies data on the profit potential of a new service or branch but also directs the total advertising program, serves as a source of competitive intelligence, and conducts sales training. It translates Maslow's theory of human needs into sales messages aimed at every segment of the bank's market. It puts into action management's recognition of and strong commitment to the principle that all business decisions must be made after consideration has been given to profit factors and customer wants and needs.

The word "salesman" is no longer derogatory; the effective banker *is* the salesman who motivates customers to use the bank. In money-market cities where many competing banks coexist, there may be few or no real differences in the range of services offered. If the delivery of these services is timely, thorough, and accurate in each case, the bank that achieves a dominant position in any one area can usually point to the effectiveness of its marketing program as the reason.

One major bank identified three problems in this area as it attempted to restructure its marketing effort to meet changing conditions:

[3] In Prochnow and Prochnow, *op. cit.*, p. 381.

[4] Howard D. Crosse and George H. Hempel, *Management Policies for Commercial Banks*, 2nd ed., Englewood Cliffs, NJ, Prentice-Hall, 1973, p. 281.

> Calling officers didn't have time to make the sales calls they should; they weren't motivated to sell and many who were didn't really know how to sell; and current customers didn't use many of the bank's services.[5]

The problems were solved first by organizational restructuring so that business development officers could concentrate on selling and second by instituting programs designed to train the staff in selling skills, self-motivation, cross-selling, and interpersonal relationships and communications. The new world of banking requires individuals with these qualities, who have understood and applied the role of human relations in their cultivation of customers. By empathizing with their clients they can focus the services of the bank on the customers' needs and thus enhance the image of the bank.[6]

This quasi-educational aspect of the marketing function is of particular importance with regard to the EFTS field. Many consumer reservations, uncertainties, and fears have been clearly identified. Those programs that appear highly desirable from the bank's viewpoint cannot be successfully introduced unless a full-scale effort results in convincing the consumer that they benefit him or her as well as the institution itself. The new world of banking must mirror the new world of American society. Today's consumer group includes many individuals who are more sophisticated, affluent, and receptive to change; banks must prove to them that the new systems are secure, cost-effective, and accurate, and are not designed to lessen individuality or remove personal control over banking transactions. The danger to the bank lies in "concentrating on the technology and forgetting about the user, upon whom the real success of EFTS will depend."[7]

In banking's new world, the three traditional and basic functions—accepting and handling deposits, processing payments, and extending credit—remain essentially unchanged. It is the scope, type, and substructure of those functions that have been modified and expanded.

The type of deposit predominating in commercial banking today is

[5] J. Wilmer Mirandon, "Mobilizing for Personal Selling," *Burroughs Clearing House*, June 1973, p. 20.

[6] Ray C. Brewster, "More Psychology in Selling," *Harvard Business Review*, July-August 1953, p. 91.

[7] George C. White, Jr., "Electronic Funds Transfer Services (EFTS) Update," speech delivered to New York City Chapter, Bank Administration Institute, Conference of March 16, 1978.

not the large, relatively inactive checking account that was typical in the past. The main thrust is in the time deposit area, which creates direct interest expense; demand deposits generally remain with banks only to the extent that they support credit facilities and/or compensate for various services. The emphasis placed by customers and banks alike on enhanced cash management services results, somewhat paradoxically, in on-line terminal systems that allow the financial officers of a corporation, unit of government, correspondent bank, or institution to monitor demand deposit balances more closely than ever before and to draw down and invest excess funds.

The same point may be made in the payments area. One of the most significant changes in banking in recent years reflects the types of payment mechanisms used by the institutions themselves in their interbank movement of funds and by their customers in disbursing. Even though the total "checkless" society, as it was first envisioned, may never arrive, EFT services still hold the potential to become the most important development in terms of total impact on the banking system.

Finally, in the credit area the changes that have occurred involve the type and scope of loans made to accommodate the total customer market. The new emphasis on personal overdraft privileges, the use of bank cards to incur debt, the expansion of international leasing and factoring operations, the formation of syndicates with foreign banks to provide large loans in many parts of the world, and the acquisitions by BHCs of small loan companies exemplify this.

THE IMPACT OF EFTS

Two of the Hunt Commission's co-directors have stressed the point that EFTS will not only affect the deposit, payment, and credit functions, but will have an impact on the geographic and numerical composition of the banking industry:

> Businesses will be able to utilize the services of banks at considerable distances . . . thus permitting even small businesses to utilize banks which are not in the same community. This will intensify competition in bank markets . . . [and] raises the question of the continued viability of the thousands of small banks which are now geographically protected.[8]

[8] Donald P. Jacobs and Almarin Phillips, "Hunt Proposals," *American Banker*, February 5, 1975, p. 4.

It is the last point that is likely to create extended controversy in the new world of banking, thus inhibiting further implementation of EFTS. If banking across state lines becomes possible through the use of on-line terminals, the customer in a given community will have complete access to banks in major money-market centers and will no longer have to depend on the limited resources of local institutions. The advantages of a unique location may disappear, and Paul Nadler[9] has predicted a significant reduction in the future number of banking organizations, with the survivors being those larger institutions that have learned to meet a new set of complex customer needs.

If current regulatory constraints are relaxed so that banks enjoy the same freedom from which savings and loan associations and nonbank competitors (e.g., American Express) now benefit, customers will find that trips to the bank are no longer necessary; many types of transactions will be initiated through terminals in airports, supermarkets, and other convenient locations. For corporations the banks may assume an even larger role in processing receivables and payables, including expanded direct deposit activity if businesses can be induced to use electronic funds transfers in lieu of checks.[10]

Physically, in the new world of banking the institution itself may bear little or no resemblance to many of today's structures. The high-rent locations, Gothic architecture, vaulted ceilings, and large open spaces will be replaced by far more functional, less expensive minibranches, storefront facilities, and automated installations. Existing networks of branches, in states that permit them, may undergo a substantial reduction as consolidations take place.

MANAGEMENT FOR THE FUTURE

The past is known and has been recorded. The present has been analyzed. Can the future be foreseen with any degree of certainty? If commercial banks are to attain their dual objectives of generating profits through providing Full Service banking to the total marketplace, what are the most significant challenges they appear likely to face? How may

[9]In Prochnow and Prochnow, *op. cit.*, p. 388.
[10]George C. White, Jr., "Innovations in Cash Management," *Bank Administration*, March 1975, p. 58.

those objectives be attained? What actions and reactions can one expect?

A synthesis of all that has been said and written on these topics indicates that there will be an interplay of several critical elements if continued growth and profitability are to take place. Four specific abilities will be required.

Ability to Meet the Challenge of Foreign Banks

Foreign banks now make more than 15 percent of all large commercial loans in the United States; in New York and California, where their presence in felt most strongly, the proportion is almost 30 percent. The consummated or pending acquisitions of domestic banks by foreign institutions in 1979 represent the transfer of over $25 billion in assets away from American ownership. The incredible concentration of wealth among OPEC members leads to the belief that they will seek to acquire more American banks as investments. Because accounting standards differ from one country to another, the true financial condition of a foreign bank is not always easy to determine. Last, and perhaps most important, foreign banks continue to enjoy a freedom denied to domestic institutions in that they can offer Full Service banking across state lines. The International Banking Act of 1978 restricts future actions, but does little to remove what is already in place.

Senator John Heinz of the Banking and Finance Committee proposed a moratorium in 1979 on all further takeover attempts by foreign banks or interests in order to allow for detailed Congressional study of all the implications of this question.[11]

The question of reciprocal action by foreign governments if American laws were enacted to curtail the present trend has frequently been raised in the past. Today the threat of such action appears less important than the threat of a concentration of domestic banking assets in the hands of foreign owners, whose interests may be in conflict with our own.

Ability to Meet the Challenge of Nonbank Institutions

Savings and loan associations, governed by a separate federal agency and frequently unhampered by the state laws that restrict commercial

[11] John Heinz 3d, "The Threat of Foreign Banking," *The New York Times*, July 22, 1979, p. Bus-14.

banks, have shown an ability to attract business away from the latter. Recently several of them have "gone public" to gain the capital that enables them to compete even more effectively.[12]

A client today can telephone Fidelity Management and Research Company in Boston on a toll-free number, buy shares in a daily-income money-market fund, and have the privilige of withdrawal through a free checking account.[13] Merrill Lynch's "cash management" service for consumers has most of the characteristics of a commercial banking relationship.[14] Approximately seventy-five of these money-market funds now are in operation; they handle some $40 billion in assets and are attracting funds at the rate of $175 million per day.[15] John Heimann, Comptroller of the Currency, has described the inroads made on the banking industry by the credit unions, whose assets now exceed $62 billion.[16] Retailers, with Sears Roebuck as the bellwether, are aggressively offering some of the services over which commercial banks once held the exclusive franchise.[17]

The only logical action banks can take in this regard requires a concerted and continous effort to seek legislative relief. As in the foreign bank situation, this should not take the form of a vendetta in which reprisals are sought against the competition. Rather, it should clearly and forcefully make the point that current regulatory and antitrust constraints are, in many cases, anachronisms that can no longer be justified.

It is not unreasonable to propose that America's major corporations, which have traditionally relied on commercial banks to meet their credit needs and provide them with basic services, be invited to support them in this effort. If disintermediation from the commercial banking system is allowed to continue in its present proportions, a situation may eventually develop in which the banks can no longer accommodate these clients. In that event, it is certain that neither a Merrill Lynch, a credit union, nor a Sears Roebuck will be able to fill the vacuum.

[12]"The S & Ls: The Conversion Era," *Financial World*, July 1, 1979, p. 38.

[13]"Everyone is Stepping into Everyone Else's Turf," *Forbes*, April 16, 1979, p. 134.

[14]Robert A. Bennett, "Merrill Vies for Bank Customers," *The New York Times*, July 9, 1979.

[15]"Mania for Money Market Funds," *Time*, November 5, 1979, p. 83.

[16]John G. Heimann with Richard B. Miller, "A Conversation with the Comptroller," *The Bankers Magazine*, January-February 1979, p. 30.

[17]Stuart Greenbaum, "The Future of Commercial Banking," *American Banker*, June 12, 1979, p. 4.

The banks' ability to diversify into new, financially oriented areas is the key to the maintenance of their role as the pillars of the economy. If they are able to become, or are desirous of becoming, the type of "financial supermaket" once predicted as their future format, they will find that this concept of an institution offering a complete range of congeneric services has already gained some degree of acceptance among the public; in 1972, 45 percent of the respondents to a nationwide study said they would either be "very interested" or "somewhat interested."[18]

If banks are to attempt to enlist a greater degree of public support in their efforts to be given greater freedom and flexibility, they must recognize the opposition they can expect to encounter. Fears of unsure concentration of power in the hands of a relatively small number of banking giants, potential litigation, and the public awareness of major bank failures and problems in recent years must be considered.

Ability to Market EFTS Effectively

The network of Automated Clearing Houses has been established and its component units interconnected. The in-bank hardware and software are, for the most part, now in place at banks throughout the country. All that is needed is a customer base large enough to make EFTS systems flourish; yet the American marketplace, with but a few significant exceptions, has remained basically aloof or openly opposed.

Those significant exceptions include the Hinky Dinky project and the federal government's programs for Social Security disbursements and Air Force payrolls. These successes have been publicized, but so have the failures, such as that experienced by a California savings and loan that found it necessary to close down its 130-terminal system and abandon the experiment.[19]

The new world of banking requires a more effective marketing campaign, through which the banks will be able to overcome consumer fears of loss of privacy and control. This campaign will have to be a positive one, placing its stress on the direct benefits to the user. It is self-defeating to try to force-feed a system to a public that has strong reservations

[18]Louis Harris, *The Second Study: The American Public's and Community Opinion Leaders' Views of Banks and Bankers in 1972*, Philadelphia, The Foundation for Full Service Banks, 1972, p. 118.

[19]Robert A. Eisenbeis, "A Framework for Evaluating the Debate over EFTS," in *Conference on Bank Structure and Competition*, April 1977, p. 303

about the system, or to market it by emphasizing only its advantages to the banks. The sophisticated consumer today is prone to ask the question, "What's in it for me?" As the ranks of competitors proliferate and their efforts become even more aggressive, the consumer has a new freedom of choice. If commercial banks are to attract consumer business, there must be strong motivating factors that can come only from an educational program.

To counter that competition and market their own systems, banks must create an image of themselves as innovative—a quality they have so long and so often been said to lack. Thrift institutions, money market funds, credit unions, and retailers have achieved their gains at the expense of the banks by being innovators, by identifying customer needs and wants and responding to them, and by offering new services on a cost-effective basis. Their examples must be followed if the banks are to react effectively.

In the new world of banking funds do not and will not steadily flow into the system on an automatic, unsolicited basis. Creativity and flexibility must play a greater role. There will always be observers, some of whom may occupy positions of authority in regulatory agencies, who will look at the manner in which banks are preparing payrolls for companies, handling rent and tax collections, leasing all types of equiment, and performing a host of peripheral services and will say, "But that isn't banking!" Yet in each of these cases there *is* some form of relevance to banking functions.[20]

These observers would undoubtedly look askance at a new system known as *Prestel*[21], which combines a type of receiver with a television to give the user access, in his or her home or office, to a huge data bank of computerized information. In Great Britain, Barclays Bank has adapted this system to allow consumers to enter information through the terminal to apply for a loan. The next adaptation may include a printout, on the television screen, of a store's catalogue listing; the user could then initiate purchases through the terminal and have them immediately debited to a bank account.[22] Certainly this represents a major departure from the traditional banking function, but that fact cannot be used to

[20]Paul Nadler, *Commercial Banking in the Economy*, 2nd ed., New York, Random House, 1973, p. 202.

[21]" 'Prestel': A Glimpse at the Future," *American Banker*, May 22, 1979, p. 7.

[22]"TV Turns to Print," *Newsweek*, July 30, 1979, p. 74.

justify ignoring or underestimating it. If American commercial banks do not seize the opportunity to introduce the service and market it wherever feasible and legally possible, there is no doubt that some form of competitor will.

Ability to Organize and Staff to Meet Future Needs

In the new world of banking, there must be a basic recognition of the fact that the systems of internal organization and personnel administration that served to get the job done in the past are no longer valid. The marketplace, the work force, and the technology that makes new services possible have all experienced tremendous change; banks must keep pace with them and adapt to them.

There must be a willingness to restructure internally and to revise traditional philosophies in order to address specific market segments. Equivalent willingness will break down the bank's former strong parochialism so that the skills and expertise of individuals from specialized nonbanking areas can be introduced and utilized, for example, in areas such as industrial engineering and psychology, data processing, cost accounting, marketing, and corporate planning.

Banks must be ready to implement expanded systems of management information so that decision making is simplified and expedited. Given the abilities of modern computers, there is no reason for a bank to operate without knowing fully the profitability of each branch or service.

Finally, new procedures in human resources management are necessary if banks are to attract, develop, motivate, and retain those individuals who will best be able to respond to the challenges facing the industry.

THE DYNAMICS OF CHANGE

Resistance to change is a common trait among humans. There is an innate tendency not to disturb the status quo and ask why any new technique or approach is necessary. In actuality, however, change is the real enemy only of those who cannot accept and adjust to it. History is replete with evidence of this in organisms and organizations alike. The dinosaurs were unable to cope with change and went out of existence. Individuals who remain hopelessly tied to the past, and cannot relate to the present, fail, inside and outside the job environment. American railroads could neither see the implications of change nor respond to it, and they lost their status as a result. The lessons are there, plainly written, for commercial bankers to see and understand.

Every contemporary topic, issue, and problem in banking relates to this same principle. If banks are to avoid going the way of the dinosaurs and railroads, they must anticipate change and be in a position to capitalize on it. Their role must be active, not merely reactive. This is a formidable challenge, but one that carries with it an opportunity and a potential reward that may well be greater than any provided in the past.

BIBLIOGRAPHY

Austin, Douglas V., and Booker, Gene S., *Modern Techniques in Bank Management*, Boston, Warren, Gorham & Lamont, 1969.

Baker, James C., and Bradford, M. Gerald, *American Banks Abroad*, New York, Praeger, 1974.

Berliner, William M., *Managerial and Supervisory Practice: Cases and Principles*, 7th, Homewood, IL, Richard D. Irwin, 1979.

Candilis, Wray O., *The Future of Commercial Banking*, New York, Praeger, 1975.

Coombs, Charles A., *The Arena of International Finance*, New York, Wiley, 1976.

Corson, John J., and Steiner, George A., *Measuring Business's Social Performance: The Corporate Social Audit*, New York, Committee for Economic Development, 1974.

Crosse, Howard D., and Hempel, George H., *Management Policies for Commercial Banks*, 2nd., Ed.

Englewood Cliffs, NJ, Prentice-Hall 1973.

Drucker, Peter F., *Management: Tasks, Responsibilities, Processes*, New York, Harper & Row, 1974.

The Practice of Management, New York, Harper & Row, 1954.

Preparing Tomorrow's Business Leaders Today, Englewood Cliffs, NJ, Prentice-Hall, 1969.

Franks, J. R., and Broyles, J. E., *Modern Managerial Finance*, Chichester, Wiley, 1979.

Fulmer, Robert M., *The New Management*, 2nd ed., New York, Macmillan, 1978.

Practical Human Relations, Homewood, IL, Richard D. Irwin, 1977.

Glueck, William F., *Personnel: A Diagnostic Approach*, rev. ed., Dallas, Business Publications, 1978.

Harris, Louis, *The Second Study: The American Public's and Community Opinion Leaders' Views of Banks and Bankers in 1972*, Philadelphia, The Foundation for Full Service Banks, 1972.

Hawke, John D., Jr., and Petersen, Neal L., *The New Community Reinvestment Act and Consumer Credit Rules: Regulatory Compliance and Bank Marketing*, New York, Law & Business, Harcourt Brace Jovanovich, 1979.

Heller, Pauline B., *Handbook of Federal Bank Holding Company Law*, New York, Law Journal Press, 1976.

Hendrickson, Robert A., *The Cashless Society*, New York, Dodd, Mead, 1972.

Herzberg, Frederick, Mausner, Bernard, and Snyderman, Barbara B., *The Motivation to Work*, New York, Wiley, 1959.

Humble, John W., *How to Manage by Objectives*, New York, AMACOM, A Division of American Management Associations, 1972.

Hunt, Alfred L., *Corporate Cash Management and Electronic Funds Transfers*, New York, AMACOM, A division of American Management Associations, 1978.

Hutchinson, Harry D., *Money, Banking, and the United States Economy*, 4th ed., Englewood Cliffs, NJ, Prentice-Hall, 1980.

Jacoby, Neil H., *Corporate Power and Social Responsibility*, New York, Macmillan, 1973.

Jessee, Michael A., and Seelig, Steven A., *Bank Holding Companies and the Public Interest*, Lexington, MA, Lexington Books (D. C. Heath), 1977.

Kepner, Charles H., and Tregoe, Benjamin B., *The Rational Manager*, New York, McGraw-Hill, 1965.

Lamb, W. Ralph, *Group Banking: A Form of Banking Concentration and Control in the United States*, New Brunswick, NJ, Rutgers University Press, 1961.

Lundborg, Louis B., *Future Without Shock*, New York, Norton 1974.

Maslow, Abraham, *Motivation and Personality*, New York, Harper & Row, 1954.

Mason, John M., *Financial Management of Commercial Banks*, Boston, Warren, Gorham & Lamont, 1979.

Mayer, Martin, *The Bankers*, New York, David McKay Co., 1974.

McGregor, Douglas, *The Human Side of Enterprise*, New York, McGraw-Hill, 1960.

McKie, James W. (Ed.), *Social Responsibility and the Business Predicament*, Washington, Brookings Institution, 1974.

Nadler, Paul S., *Commercial Banking in the Economy*, 2nd ed., New York, Random House, 1973.

Prochnow, Herbert V. (Ed.), *The One-Bank Holding Company*, Chicago, Rand McNally, 1969.

and Prochnow, Herbert V., Jr., (Eds), *The Changing World of Banking*, New York, Harper & Row, 1974.

Reed, Edward W., Cotter, Richard V., Gill, Edward K., and Smith, Richard K., *Commercial Banking*, Englewood Cliffs, NJ, Prentice-Hall, 1976.

Robichek, Alexander A., Coleman, Alan B., and Hempel, George H., *Management of Financial Institutions: Notes and Cases*, Hinsdale, IL, Dryden, 1976.

Rockefeller, David, *Creative Management in Banking*, New York, McGraw-Hill, 1964.

Roeber, Richard J. C., *The Organization in a Changing Environment*, Reading, MA, Addison-Wesley, 1973.

Russell, Thomas, *The Economics of Bank Credit Cards*, New York, Praeger, 1975.

Teplitz, Paul V., *Trends Affecting the U.S. Banking System*, Cambridge, MA, Cambridge Research Institute, 1976.

Thompson, Thomas W., Berry, Leonard L., and Davidson, Phillip H., *Banking Tomorrow: Managing Markets Through Planning*, New York, Van Nostrand Reinhold, 1978.

Wood, Oliver G., Jr., *Commercial Banking: Practice and Policy*, New York, D. Van Nostrand, 1978.

INDEX